FATHERS
as
PATRIARCHS

This book is dedicated to my youngest daughter, Kenon. It is my earnest desire that she will select a mate who will be a true patriarch in their home.

ISBN: 0-929985-60-5

Grant Von Harrison

FATHERS
as
PATRIARCHS

Keepsake Paperbacks
Orem, Utah

CONTENTS

Introduction

In the general priesthood meeting in October 1985, President Ezra Taft Benson admonished modern-day fathers to follow the example of Book of Mormon fathers in rearing their children. Two years later in another general priesthood meeting, he spoke specifically to fathers regarding their patriarchal duties. The fact that a prophet of God addressed the topic of fathers as patriarchs twice in two years suggests the Lord is vitally concerned about fathers effectively performing their patriarchal duties.

In his opening remarks at the October general conference in 1988, President Benson challenged church members to consider prayerfully ways they could bring the Book of Mormon more fully into their lives. He went on to say, "I have a vision of the whole church getting nearer to God by abiding the precepts of the Book of Mormon." Then he made a prophetic statement: "I have a vision of homes alerted" as a result of the Book of Mormon (*Ensign*, Nov. 1988, pp. 4-6). Over the years President Ezra Taft Benson has specified the following blessings your family will realize if you regularly study the Book of Mormon:

- The spirit of reverence will increase in your home.
- Mutual respect and consideration for other family members will grow.
- The spirit of contention will depart from your home.
- You will be able to counsel your children with greater love and wisdom.
- Your family will develop a closer relationship with Christ.
- Your ability to teach your children will be magnified.
- Your ability to receive personal revelation to bless the lives of the members of your family will increase.
- Faith, love, and charity will abound in your home.

These remarks and promises by President Benson make it very clear that the Book of Mormon has the power to help you strengthen your family.

In his opening remarks in the 1988 October general conference, President Benson encouraged church writers to write books dealing with the Book of Mormon. I have written this book with a sincere desire that it will further the cause of Zion by helping fathers view the scriptures, especially the Book of Mormon, coupled with the teachings of modern-day prophets, as their handbooks in learning to be effective patriarchs to their families.

The primary focus of the book is to examine passages from the Book of Mormon that depict fathers performing their duties as patriarchs in behalf of their families. These examples from the Book of Mormon, combined with other scriptures and the teachings of modern-day prophets, are used to portray the duties of a father as a patriarch. I feel the scriptures and quotes are the most important parts of the book. The benefits of this book may be limited unless the scriptures and quotes are read very carefully.

1

You Have a Holy Calling

The calling of a patriarch is one of the most revered offices associated with the Melchizedek Priesthood. Men called as stake patriarchs are men who have demonstrated over years of church service their special receptiveness to inspiration and have earned the esteem and respect of those that know them.

As young men grow up in the church, they are taught about the role of the stake patriarch and are encouraged to receive their patriarchal blessings before they go on their missions. Young men generally receive some instruction regarding patriarchal blessings each year after they receive the priesthood. However, some of the same young men grow up and become fathers and have very little awareness of their role and calling as a patriarch to their own families. Consequently, some do not valiantly perform their patriarchal duties. Elder L. Tom Perry has warned that divorce, infidelity, dishonesty, the use of drugs, deterioration of family life, loss of identity, instability, and unhappiness result when fathers fail to perform their patriarchal duties (*Ensign*, Nov. 1977, p. 62).

Duly Ordained Fathers Are Patriarchs

Beginning with Father Adam, blessing members of their family has always been the right of duly ordained fathers. A father who holds the Melchizedek Priesthood and has entered into the patriarchal order of celestial marriage has the authority to bless his wife and children as a patriarch. As a father, you should approach your calling as a patriarch as conscientiously as do stake patriarchs. Both are holy callings.

The Importance of Your Patriarchal Calling

Of all the callings associated with the Melchizedek Priesthood, the calling of a father as a patriarch is the most important. In a general priesthood meeting in 1987, President Ezra Taft Benson stressed this point:

> Fathers, yours is an eternal calling from which you are never released. Callings in the Church, as important as they are, by their very nature are only for a period of time, and then an appropriate release takes place. But a father's calling is eternal, and its importance transcends time. It is a calling for both time and eternity. President Harold B. Lee truly stated that "the most important of the Lord's work that you [fathers] will ever do will be the work you do within the walls of your own home. Home teaching, bishopric's work, and other Church duties are all important, but the most important work is within the walls of your home." (*Ensign*, Nov. 1987, p. 48)

The following statement by President N. Eldon Tanner summarizes the magnitude of your responsibility as a patriarch to your family:

> It is a joyous privilege and blessing, and a heavy responsibility, to be the father and the patriarchal head of a family, with the challenge to teach and prepare its members to go back into the presence of their Heavenly Father, where the family can continue to enjoy eternal life together. (*Ensign*, June 1987, p. 2)

In light of the far-reaching implications of the responsibilities associated with fatherhood, you should resolve to exercise your rights and authority as a patriarch in your home.

Catch the Vision of Your Calling

Elder J. Richard Clarke related the following experience in general conference:

> Many years ago, in this Tabernacle, I heard Elder Sterling Sill recognize the men who had performed the essential priesthood ordinances listed on his membership record. I suddenly realized that my father's name did not appear on my record. He had not been active in the Church while I was growing up but had since become a faithful high priest.
>
> Returning home from conference, I brooded about this, feeling deprived. I telephoned my father and said, "Dad, I'd like to ask you a favor. You can do something for me that no other living person can do. I would like a father's blessing." He hesitated and said, "Well, we'll see, the next time you come to Rexburg."
>
> I persisted. To my knowledge, he had never given a father's blessing before, and he was nervous. At the age of eighty-four, he placed his quivering hands upon my head. And this son will never forget the supreme joy of hearing a proud father pour out his heart in a blessing—a blessing which will be held sacred and cherished not because of its eloquence but because it came from my father. I hope, brethren, that you will not deny your children this choice experience. (*Ensign*, May 1989, p. 61)

This account illustrates how meaningful it is to a son or daughter when a father exercises his patriarchal keys in their behalf. However, it also illustrates another reality: some fathers, for various reasons, do not exercise their patriarchal keys often enough.

Unfortunately, some fathers have a very limited vision of their authority as a patriarch. When this proves the case, fathers fail to take full advantage of their rights as a patriarch in dealing with their children. All too often, the only time some fathers speak as a patriarch is when formal priesthood ordinances are performed (i.e., giving a child a name or confirming a child a member of the church). Ideally, you should speak as a patriarch on a regular basis in your dealings with your children—not only on those occasions when priesthood ordinances are performed.

In recent years, priesthood manuals have addressed the role of fathers as patriarchs more frequently. In spite of this increased focus in Melchizedek Priesthood manuals, some fathers still fail to adequately discharge their responsibilities as patriarchs. As a general rule, a father's negligence in exercising his patriarchal keys is the result of a lack of understanding, not a lack of desire. Most fathers are very sincere in their desire to assist and bless their children in any way they can.

The Role of Scriptures and the Teachings of Modern-Day Prophets

The scriptures, especially the Book of Mormon, coupled with the teachings of modern-day prophets, will instruct you in how to perform your patriarchal duties. Some of the greatest examples of fathers as patriarchs are recorded in the scriptures, particularly the Book of Mormon. The Book of Mormon, more than any other book, will help you catch the vision of your calling as a patriarch (see D&C 33:16). The Book of Mormon was written under inspiration for our day (see 1 Nephi 19:23; Mormon 8:35). This is why the Book of Mormon should be your primary handbook regarding your holy calling as a patriarch.

Foreseeing the needs of our day, the Lord inspired ancient prophets to include examples of righteous fathers performing their patriarchal duties when he had them compile the Book of Mormon. Consequently, over five hundred verses in the Book of Mormon deal specifically with teachings, counsel, blessings and letters of fathers to their children. (These verses, and other related references, are listed at the back of this book.) As you make a careful study of how righteous fathers in the Book of Mormon dealt with their children, your vision of your authority as a patriarch will be enhanced significantly.

A primary example would be Father Lehi. Lehi truly had a vision of his calling as a patriarch to his children. You can learn a great deal regarding your authority as a patriarch from studying Lehi's life. When Lehi recorded his visions, dreams, and prophecies, he was writing for the benefit of his posterity (see 1 Nephi 1:16; 2 Nephi 4:2). In contrast, his son Nephi was commanded to write for all future generation (see 1 Nephi 1:3; 1 Nephi 19:3; 1 Nephi 6:4; 1 Nephi 9:3). This helps explain why the Lord used the writings of Nephi when the Book of Mormon was compiled. Fortunately, Nephi quotes his father extensively in his record, so modern-day fathers can profit from Lehi's example.

There is no indication Lehi was a prophet prior to the first vision Nephi recounts in his record. Lehi more likely was a man who held the Melchizedek Priesthood and was an active member of a local congregation. But most important, he was a conscientious father who understood his authority as a patriarch. This is very evident in Nephi's writings about his father.

It was a prayer Lehi offered in behalf of his family that led to the vision described in Nephi's account. Nephi described his father's experience as follows:

> Wherefore it came to pass that my father, Lehi, as he went forth prayed unto the Lord, yea, even with all his heart, in behalf of his people.
>
> And it came to pass as he prayed unto the Lord, there came a pillar of fire and dwelt upon a rock before him; and he saw and heard much; and because of the things which he saw and heard he did quake and tremble exceedingly. (1 Nephi 1:5-6)

It is important to note that Lehi prayed in behalf of his family (his people). When Nephi refers to the Jews generally, he calls them "the people" (see 1 Nephi 1:18). As a result of this mighty prayer of a father as a patriarch, the Lord prepared the way for Lehi and his family to be led to a promised land (see 1 Nephi 2:20). In this way, Lehi and his family were spared when Jerusalem was later destroyed.

Apparently Lehi was concerned about the consequences that the sinful conditions in Jerusalem would bring on his family. From Nephi's account, it is apparent that Laman and Lemuel had been influenced by the prevailing beliefs of the day:

> Now this he spake because of the stiffneckedness of Laman and Lemuel; for behold they did murmur in many things against their father, because he was a visionary man, and had led them out of the land of Jerusalem, to leave the land of their inheritance, and their gold, and their silver, and their precious things, to perish in the wilderness. And this they said he had done because of the foolish imaginations of his heart.

> And thus Laman and Lemuel, being the eldest, did murmur against their father. And they did murmur because they knew not the dealings of that God who had created them.

> Neither did they believe that Jerusalem, that great city, could be destroyed according to the words of the prophets. And they were like unto the Jews who were at Jerusalem, who sought to take away the life of my father. (1 Nephi 2:11-13)

In our day and age, some 2500 years later, it is intriguing to consider the far-reaching effects of the prayer Lehi offered as a patriarch in behalf of his family. The Lord used the records of the descendants of Lehi, combined with the records of the Jaredites, when the Book of Mormon was compiled.

Alma's counsel to his three sons as recorded in the Book of Mormon is very indicative of how a father should deal with his children if he understands his authority as a patriarch (see Alma 36-41). There are many parallels between the recorded accounts of Lehi and Alma dealing with their children and the accounts of how other righteous fathers in the Book of Mormon dealt with their children. King Benjamin and Helaman are typical examples. Most often when we think of King Benjamin, we think of his effectiveness in governing the Nephites and his incredible ability to motivate people to live righteously. However, a father can learn a great deal about his responsibilities as a patriarch from the few verses included in the Book of Mormon regarding King Benjamin's dealings with his sons (see Mosiah 1:1-8). Even though only nine verses in the Book of Mormon talk about Helaman's relationship with two of his sons, it is very evident he understood his authority as a patriarch (see Helaman 5:5-14).

Through modern-day prophets, the Lord has given us to know that the Book of Mormon should receive special focus in our scripture study. Every father in Israel has the responsibility to study the accounts in the Book of Mormon that portray fathers as patriarchs and then to make it a practice to review these accounts prayerfully on a regular basis. President Ezra Taft Benson admonishes fathers to emulate the example of these great Book of Mormon patriarchs.

You Can Be Taught From On High

Your vision of your role as a patriarch to your children will enlarge dramatically as you study the Book of Mormon regularly. As you follow the admonition of President Ezra Taft Benson to study the Book of Mormon daily, you will be taught from on high regarding your calling as a patriarch (see D&C 84:48). Being taught from on high is a key in coming to an understanding of the power and authority you have at your disposal as a patriarch. You will not realize your full stature as patriarch to your family until you trust the Lord's promise that he will teach you regarding the covenants and authority associated with the Melchizedek Priesthood. This promise is one of the most significant promises associated with the Oath and Covenant of the Priesthood.

As you develop a more comprehensive vision of the things you have the authority to do as a patriarch, you will begin to exercise your patriarchal keys more frequently. As you do you will be blessed with inspiration from God in leading, guiding, and directing your family in righteousness. When this happens, your calling as a patriarch will become the highest priority in your life, and your family will be blessed in special ways.

On one occasion, President Spencer W. Kimball declared, "These are happy days, the days of the patriarchs" (*Ensign*, Nov. 1977, p. 4). This statement takes on special meaning as you think of your holy calling as a patriarch to your family, the most important calling in time and eternity—a call from which you will never be released.

2

Fulfill Your Sacred Responsibilities

The Lord has specified three sacred responsibilities for every father in Israel. Each of these sacred responsibilities has been given by way of commandment. Each is important. No one of the three should suffer as a result of your focus on either of the other two. As a patriarch to your family you are expected to maintain an appropriate balance in fulfilling these sacred responsibilities.

Provide for the Material Needs of Your Family

You have the sacred responsibility to provide for the material needs of your family. The Lord has been very forthright in specifying this responsibility.

> But if any provide not for his own, and especially for those of his own house, he hath denied the faith, and is worse than an infidel. (1 Timothy 5:8)

• • •

> And again, verily I say unto you, that every man who is obliged to provide for his own family, let him provide, and in nowise lose his crown; and let him labor in the church. (D&C 75:28)

• • •

Women have claim on their husbands for their main-
tenance, until their husbands are taken. (D&C 83:2)

• • •

And ye will not suffer your children that they go
hungry, or naked. (Mosiah 4:14)

Here are the words of a modern-day prophet concerning
your responsibility to provide for your family:

> You have a sacred responsibility to provide for the
> material needs of your family . . . While she cares for
> and nourishes her children at home, her husband
> earns the living for the family, which makes this
> nourishing possible. (President Ezra Taft Benson,
> *Ensign*, Nov. 1987, pp. 48-49)

Over the years church leaders have consistently stressed
that every able-bodied husband should work. Throughout the
scriptures the Lord denounces idleness (see 1 Nephi 5:24;
Ezekiel 16:49; D&C 188:124; Alma 38:12; D&C 42:42).
Beginning with Adam, the Lord has stipulated that men work
(see Genesis 3:19). From the writings of Nephi we learn that
a person who is guilty of idleness will not be happy (see 2
Nephi 5:24-27).

Unless you are physically or mentally incapacitated, there
is no excuse for your not working. At times you may have to
work at menial jobs until you find something better, but as a
patriarch you must accept the adage "Any work is better than
no work." If you are unable to find a regular job, make your
services available to ward members and other acquaintances.
Never let your pride stop you from seeking hourly work from
people you know. In some instances, hourly work for acquaintances can lead to regular employment.

Your stewardship to provide for the material needs of your
family goes beyond working on a regular basis. You also have
the responsibility to manage your earnings so you have some
savings to fall back on and a food supply in case of an emer-
gency.

In the fall of 1987 general priesthood meeting, President Ezra Taft Benson counseled fathers specifically regarding this responsibility:

> Fathers, another vital aspect of providing for the material needs of your family is the provision you should be making for your family in case of an emergency. Family preparedness has been a long-established welfare principle. It is even more urgent today.
>
> I ask you earnestly, have you provided for your family a year's supply of food, clothing, and, where possible, fuel? The revelation to produce and store food may be as essential to our temporal welfare today as boarding the ark was to the people in the days of Noah.
>
> Also, are you living within your income and saving a little?
>
> Are you honest with the Lord in the payment of your tithes? Living this divine law will bring both spiritual and material blessings.
>
> Yes, brethren, as fathers in Israel you have a great responsibility to provide for the material needs of your family and to have the necessary provisions in case of emergency. (*Ensign*, Nov. 1987, p. 49)

Unless a father who is capable is willing to work on a regular basis to provide for his family, he will lose the spirit of his calling as a patriarch. When this happens, there is always the danger children will lose respect for their father. A father's power to influence his children for good is minimal if they do not respect him. The situation is further compounded when a father loses his self-confidence as a result of not adequately providing for the material needs of his family. Work is important to human happiness and self-esteem as well as productivity. Commenting on the importance of work, President Spencer W. Kimball made this profound statement: "Work has spiritual dimensions. Work is a spiritual necessity as well as an economic necessity. Our pioneer forebears understood this." (*Teachings of Spencer W. Kimball*, p. 359)

Some fathers fall prey to self-deception and form an attitude that they can make money without having a regular job.
When a man succumbs to this way of thinking, he is prone to
get involved in one get-rich scheme after another. If a father
fails to see the error in his thinking, he will go years without a
regular job, thinking the next get-rich scheme is going to be
successful. Any father who has fallen victim to this pattern of
thinking should heed the advice of President Spencer W.
Kimball:

> Success requires diligent effort. Success is not like
> manna that falls every working day alike on the
> worker and the shiftless, on the resourceful one and
> the careless one. Success is reserved for those who
> work at it, those not afraid of the midnight oil.
> (*Teachings of Spencer W. Kimball*, pp. 359-360)

• • •

> Profiting from others' weaknesses displeases God.
> Clean money is that compensation received for a full
> day's honest work. It is that reasonable pay for faith-
> ful service. It is that fair profit from the sale of goods,
> commodities, or service. It is that income received
> from transactions where all parties profit. . . .

> Compromise money is filthy, graft money is unclean,
> profit and commissions on the sale of worthless
> goods, contaminated as is the money gained from
> other deceptions, excessive pricing, oppression to the
> poor, and compensation which is not fully earned. I
> feel strongly that men who accept wages or salary and
> do not give commensurate time, energy, devotion,
> and service are receiving money that is not clean.
> Certainly those who deal in the forbidden are recipi-
> ents of filthy lucre. (*Teachings of Spencer W. Kimball*,
> p. 356)

• • •

> With regard to all phases of our lives, I believe that
> men should help themselves. They should plow and
> plant and cultivate and harvest and not expect their

14

faith to bring them bread. (*Teachings of Spencer W. Kimball*, p. 370)

You will not be susceptible to the enticement of get-rich schemes if you have a clear understanding of the meaning of the abundant life referred to in the scriptures. The abundant life the Lord speaks of in the scriptures has very little to do with the acquisition of material things. President Spencer W. Kimball has provided a very clear definition of what constitutes an abundant life:

> The abundant life noted in the scriptures is the spiritual sum that is arrived at by the multiplying of our service to others and by investing our talents in service to God and to man. (*Teachings of Spencer W. Kimball*, p. 352)

When your life is in harmony with the gospel of Jesus Christ, your family will experience joy and contentment, even if you cannot afford luxuries. Contentment is not tied to material things. Happiness comes from within; it is not the product of things. Satan would like you to believe otherwise, but you should never lose sight of the following fundamental truth expressed by President Spencer W. Kimball:

> We . . . live in a wonderfully good world where the things which really bring us unbounded joy may still be had in rich abundance if we are willing to pay the price, and that price is expressed not in money but in effort. (*Teachings of Spencer W. Kimball*, p. 353)

You have the absolute assurance that as you make an honest effort in performing your sacred responsibility to provide for your family, the Lord will sustain you in your efforts. You should strive to exercise faith in this promise each and every day. Otherwise, your lack of faith limits the Lord in assisting you in your efforts to provide for your family. Just as "faith without works is dead," work or effort without corresponding faith will limit your capacity to provide for your family.

Love and Sustain Your Wife

As a husband, you are commanded to love and sustain your wife. The apostle Paul commented on this sacred responsibility in his epistle to the Ephesians:

Husbands, love your wives, even as Christ also loved the church, and gave himself for it;

That he might sanctify and cleanse it with the washing of water by the word,

That he might present it to himself a glorious church, not having spot, or wrinkle, or any such thing; but that it should be holy and without blemish.

So ought men to love their wives as their own bodies. He that loveth his wife loveth himself.

For no man ever yet hated his own flesh; but nourisheth and cherisheth it, even as the Lord the church:

For we are members of his body, of his flesh, and of his bones.

For this cause shall a man leave his father and mother, and shall be joined unto his wife, and they two shall be one flesh. (Ephesians 5:25-31)

In latter-day revelation, the Lord speaks again of this sacred responsibility. You are commanded to love your wives in the same way you love God.

Thou shalt love thy wife with all thy heart, and shalt cleave unto her and none else. (D&C 42:22)

Commenting on this commandment, President Ezra Taft Benson said:

This kind of love can be shown for your wives in so many ways. First and foremost, nothing except God Himself takes priority over your wife in your life—not work, not recreation, not hobbies. Your wife is your precious, eternal helpmate—your companion. (*Ensign*, Nov. 1987, p. 50)

President N. Eldon Tanner gave the following counsel:

> Husbands, love your wives, honor and respect them.
> Praise them and hold them high in the estimate of
> your family. (*Ensign*, June 1977, p. 5)

You will find happiness in your marriage as you comply
with the Lord's charge to love and sustain your wife. President
Spencer W. Kimball taught a formula that guarantees happiness in marriage. Part of the formula consists of loving and
sustaining your wife. It was his position that a successful marriage is possible for any couple.

> The formula is simple; the ingredients are few,
> though there are many amplifications of each.
>
> First, there must be the proper approach toward marriage, which contemplates the selection of a spouse
> who reaches as nearly as possible the pinnacle of perfection in all the matters which are of importance to
> the individuals. And then those two parties must
> come to the altar in the temple realizing that they
> must work hard toward this successful joint living.
>
> Second, there must be a great unselfishness, forgetting self and directing all of the family life and all
> pertaining thereunto to the good of the family, subjugating self.
>
> Third, there must be continued courting and expressions of affection, kindness, and consideration to
> keep love alive and growing.
>
> Fourth, there must be a complete living of the commandments of the Lord as defined in the gospel of
> Jesus Christ.
>
> With these ingredients properly mixed and continually kept functioning, it is quite impossible for unhappiness to come, misunderstandings to continue, or
> breaks to occur. Divorce attorneys would need to
> transfer to other fields and divorce courts would be
> padlocked. (*Teachings of Spencer W. Kimball*, p. 306)

From the revealed word of the Lord and the teachings of modern-day prophets, it is very clear the Lord expects you to show your wife respect, fidelity and thoughtfulness. The bond of love between you and your wife should not be based on a physical attraction alone. It should include faith, confidence, understanding, devotion, and unselfishness. When this type of love exists between you and your wife, it will endure in times of sickness, sorrow, and disappointments as well as in times of good health and prosperity.

Other than your devotion to God, your wife's needs should receive top priority in your life. You should never place work, recreation, or hobbies before her. Otherwise, you will not be equal to the Lord's charge that you love her with all of your heart. President Ezra Taft Benson explains what it means to love your wife with all your heart:

> What does it mean to love someone with all your heart? It means to love with all your emotional feelings and with all your devotion. Surely when you love your wife with all your heart, you cannot demean her, criticize her, find fault with her, or abuse her by words, sullen behavior, or actions.
>
> What does it mean to "cleave unto her"? It means to stay close to her, to be loyal and faithful to her, to communicate with her, and to express your love for her.
>
> Love means being sensitive to her feelings and needs. She wants to be noticed and treasured. She wants to be told that you view her as lovely and attractive and important to you. Love means putting her welfare and self-esteem as a high priority in your life. (*Ensign*, Nov. 1987, p. 50)

Consistently let your wife know you are grateful she is the mother of your children. Express your gratitude to her for her efforts in helping you raise your children. Recognize her abilities and talents. Learn to counsel with her regarding your children and family plans. Follow President Benson's advice to husbands, "Don't be stingy with your means" (*Ensign*, Nov. 1987, p. 50).

Motherhood is very demanding. Unless you exert yourself there is the danger your wife will become totally consumed with her domestic responsibilities. You need to make certain your wife has time to develop herself intellectually, emotionally, socially, and spiritually. This means there will be times when you will need to tend the children and assume some of the household responsibilities. Here is the advice of a prophet:

> Remember, brethren, love can be nurtured and nourished by little tokens. Flowers on special occasions are wonderful, but so is your willingness to help with the dishes, change diapers, get up with a crying child in the night, and leave the television or the newspaper to help with the dinner. Those are the quiet ways we say "I love you" with our actions. They bring rich dividends for such little effort. (President Ezra Taft Benson, *Ensign*, Nov. 1987, p. 50)

Never lose sight of your responsibility to sustain your wife, not only in her church callings but in all of her pursuits. Strive to nourish her emotionally and spiritually and build her esteem in the eyes of your children. There will be times when your wife will need special support from you; perhaps when a child is seriously ill, or in times of other pressures in her life. The critical thing is for you to be sensitive to her needs, and then to be equal to the challenge of sustaining her according to the situation. Her well-being is your responsibility in every respect.

Be the Spiritual Leader in Your Home

Your third sacred responsibility is to help your children fill the measure of their creation, so they will be fit subjects for the kingdom of God. President Spencer W. Kimball summarized this responsibility:

We do not rear children just to please our vanity. We bring children into the world to become kings and queens, and priests and priestesses for our Lord.

Many people in the Church do not have the right concept of a child. They think that he is a personality to play with, to dress, to enjoy, to have, to hold. They never think seriously about the tremendous responsibility of developing that little spirit without earthly knowledge into a fit subject for the kingdom of God.

It is the duty of parents to so teach by example and precept that a child will fill the measure of his creation and find his way back to the glories of exaltation. (*Teachings of Spencer W. Kimball*, pp. 331-332)

He also spoke to parents about their responsibility to teach their children:

Wise parents will see to it that their teaching is orthodox, character-building, and faith-promoting.

It is the responsibility of the parents to teach their children. The Sunday School, the Primary, the MIA and other organizations of the Church play a secondary role.

The Lord . . . gave us this law: when the child is eight years of age, he should have been trained—not that he should *begin* to be trained, as many of our parents surmise.

Our Heavenly Father placed the responsibility upon parents to see that their children are well trained and well taught. (*Teachings of Spencer W. Kimball*, p. 332)

• • •

On a cold winter day most children set out for school warmly clothed. The soles of their shoes are thick, and they wear boots over them. They wear heavy coats, with scarves around their necks and mittens on their hands—all to protect them from the inclemency of the weather. But are these same children protected against the mistaken ideologies and ideas of

other youth and the temptations of the day?
(*Teachings of Spencer W. Kimball*, p. 332)

• • •

What inner strength would be in every person if he
knew the Master and His teachings were indeed his
great source of guidance, his great source of correct
example, his great source of help! That is our prime
goal in all our teaching in the home. (*Teachings of
Spencer W. Kimball*, p. 333)

Even though the Lord has charged you and your wife joint-
ly with the responsibility to train your children, He expects
you to be the spiritual leader in your home. You have the primary responsibility to give your children direction, establish
rules, and deal with discipline. Your wife can assist you in
every respect, but you should never relinquish to your wife
the overall responsibility associated with training your children. The Lord expects you to be the "head" of your family in
the same way Jesus Christ stands at the head of his church.

In a general priesthood meeting, President Ezra Taft
Benson instructed fathers on their sacred responsibility to be
the spiritual leader in their home.

The powerful effect of righteous fathers in setting an
example, disciplining and training, nurturing and
loving is vital to the spiritual welfare of his children.
With love in my heart for the fathers in Israel, may I
suggest ten specific ways that fathers can give spiritual leadership to their children:

1. Give father's blessings to your children. Baptize
   and confirm your children. Ordain your sons to
   the priesthood. These will become spiritual high-
   lights in the lives of your children.

2. Personally direct family prayers, daily scripture
   reading, and weekly family home evenings. Your
   personal involvement will show your children how
   important these activities really are.

3. Whenever possible, attend Church meetings together as a family. Family worship under your leadership is vital to your children's spiritual welfare.

4. Go on daddy-daughter dates and father-and-sons' outings with your children. As a family, go on campouts and picnics, to ball games and recitals, to school programs, and so forth. Having Dad there makes all the difference.

5. Build traditions of family vacations and trips and outings. These memories will never be forgotten by your children.

6. Have regular one-on-one visits with your children. Let them talk about what they would like to. Teach them gospel principles. Teach them true values. Tell them you love them. Personal time with your children tells them where Dad puts his priorities.

7. Teach your children to work, and show them the value of working toward a worthy goal. Establishing mission funds and education funds for your children shows them what Dad considers to be important.

8. Encourage good music and art and literature in your homes. Homes that have a spirit of refinement and beauty will bless the lives of your children forever.

9. As distances allow, regularly attend the temple with your wife. Your children will then better understand the importance of temple marriage and temple vows and the eternal family unit.

10. Have your children see your joy and satisfaction in service to the Church. This can become contagious to them, so they, too, will want to serve in the Church and will love the kingdom. (*Ensign*, Nov. 1987, pp. 50-51)

As a result of the priesthood keys you enjoy as a patriarch to your family, you have the authority to conduct three meetings in your home: family councils, family home evenings, and family testimony meetings. As you hold these three meetings on a regular basis and make it a practice to interview your children, you will have ample opportunity to discharge your stewardship as the spiritual leader in your home.

In addition to these three meetings, concern yourself with the general atmosphere in your home. Strive to create an environment in your home that results in the spirit of the Lord being evident. As your children have spiritual experiences in your home, they will learn to discern the spirit of the Lord. When your children learn to discern the spirit of the Lord, they become much more capable of distinguishing between good and evil. Be consistent in admonishing your children to forsake all forms of ungodliness and evil. In order to do this, you will need to be selective in your TV viewing as a family and not allow videos, music, books or magazines in your home that are offensive to the Lord.

President Spencer W. Kimball instructed fathers as patriarchs in their home to be worthy watchmen:

> Never before have there been so many insidious influences threatening the family as today, around the world. Many of these evil influences come right into the home—through television, radio, magazines, newspapers, and other forms of literature.
>
> Brethren, as patriarchs in your homes, be worthy watchmen. Be concerned about the types of programs your family is watching on television or hearing on radio. There is so much today that is unsavory and degrading, so much that gives the impression that the old sins of Sodom and Gomorrah are the "in thing" to do today.
>
> There are magazines today publishing pictures and articles which likewise beckon to the baser instincts of men and women and young people. There are newspapers around the world which, seeking greater

circulation, boldly flaunt sex. Some of our newspapers continue to publish illustrated advertisements which are basely provocative, inviting their readers to pornographic motion pictures. It is in such advertisements and motion pictures where seeds are sown for rape, unfaithfulness, and the most repulsive of deviant sexual transgressions.

Brethren, be vigilant on what enters your home though the printed word as well as the electronic media. Guard against radio and TV programs that degrade. See that only good reading material enters your home. Subscribe to magazines which enrich the mind and uplift the soul. There are many good magazines, including our own Church periodicals, the *Ensign, New Era*, and *Friend* . . .

There are a number of daily newspapers from which to make a choice. Bring to your home the newspaper which is most compatible with the teachings and standards of the Church.

Brethren, by being alert to what enters your home, you can do much in helping your family seek that which is "virtuous, lovely, or of good report or praiseworthy." (Article of Faith 13) (*Ensign*, May 1978, p. 45)

Foreseeing the powerful influence of lasciviousness in our day, Nephi said:

For behold, at that day shall he rage in the hearts of the children of men, and stir them up to anger against that which is good.

And others will he pacify, and lull them way into carnal security, that they will say: All is well in Zion; yea, Zion prospereth, all is well—and thus the devil cheateth their souls, and leadeth them away carefully down to hell. (2 Nephi 28:20-21)

The power and influence of family prayer and scripture reading will be diminished substantially if you allow things in your home that the Lord does not condone. As you strive to keep your home free of all forms of ungodliness and evil, your children will be much less inclined to expose themselves to evil outside of the home.

As you consistently perform your responsibilities as the spiritual leader in your house, your home will be a place of happiness and joy. For the most part your home will be free of bickering, quarreling, contention, and unrighteous behavior. In contrast, the Lord has warned that if a father fails in this responsibility, Satan will have power over his children and this will be the cause of much affliction (see D&C 93:42).

You Can Change Your Children's World

Even though you cannot do much to change the world in general, you can make your children's world a much better place by making these three sacred responsibilities a priority in your life. As a patriarch you have the power within you to change your children's world. By doing so, you will do much to ensure that your children are exalted. Here are the words of a prophet:

> Oh, husbands and fathers in Israel, you can do so much for the salvation and exaltation of your families! Your responsibilities are so important.
>
> Remember your sacred calling as a father in Israel—your most important calling in time and eternity—a calling from which you will never be released.
>
> May you always provide for the material needs of your family and, with your eternal companion at your side, may you fulfill your sacred responsibility to provide the spiritual leadership in your home. (President Ezra Taft Benson, *Ensign*, Nov. 1987, p. 51)

At times the spiritual atmosphere of your home will give your children the strength to cope with the hostile world they will sometimes encounter outside of your home.

Your Children Will Be a Source of Joy

Of all the things that can bring you joy in this life, the joys associated with righteous family relations are by far the sweetest. You have the assurance that as you fulfill your sacred responsibilities as patriarch to your family, your children will be a source of joy to you. You will experience this joy when you see them strive to emulate your best characteristics, when they fulfill your highest aspirations for them, and when they express appreciation and love to you and your wife. Your crowning joy will be to see your children raising their own families in righteousness. Over the years there will be many occasions when you will rejoice as you see your children and grandchildren realizing the full measure of their creation. You will have the absolute assurance that the Lord's promises associated with your role as a patriarch are true.

3

Qualify to Exercise Patriarchal Keys

Once you understand the keys and the authority of the priesthood as they apply to your patriarchal calling, two critical prerequisites qualify you to exercise your patriarchal keys—**desire** and **worthiness.**

Desire in Behalf of Your Children

Desire in behalf of your children is a major determinant in qualifying to function as a patriarch in your home (see Alma 24:4). Throughout the scriptures the Lord repeatedly says that He grants unto men according to their desires. This is especially true in your relationship with your children.

The Lord has stipulated that fathers need to be righteous to exercise their rights as a patriarch:

> That the rights of the priesthood are inseparably con-nected with the powers of heaven, and that the pow-ers of heaven cannot be controlled nor handled only upon the principles of righteousness.
>
> That they may be conferred upon us, it is true; but when we undertake to cover our sins, or to gratify our pride, our vain ambition, or to exercise control or

dominion or compulsion upon the souls of the children of men, in any degree of unrighteousness, behold, the heavens withdraw themselves; the Spirit of the Lord is grieved; and when it is withdrawn, Amen to the priesthood or the authority of that man. (D&C 121:36-37)

At the same time the scriptures tell us that the Lord is merciful and forgiving. If you feel lacking in any respect, you need to look to the Lord for his assistance. If you will but desire to exercise your patriarchal keys, the Lord will help you qualify yourself. If you feel inadequate in any respect to perform your patriarchal duties, follow the Lord's admonition to acknowledge your weaknesses in your prayers, and then trust the Lord to magnify you in your role as a patriarch. As you do, your shortcomings will become your strengths (see Ether 12:27).

If necessary seek assistance from your home teachers, bishop, stake president, family, and friends. As you are willing to make the effort, you can be assured you will receive the direction and help you need. The Lord will assist you in qualifying to exercise your patriarchal keys according to your desires to bless your family. If you have the desire to bless your family, you will become qualified to exercise your patriarchal keys.

Assess Your Worthiness

In making judgments regarding your worthiness, be very careful. You would be wise to follow Elder Marvin J. Ashton's counsel:

> It occurs to me that there are probably hundreds or even thousands who do not understand what worthiness is. Worthiness is a process, and perfection is an eternal trek. We can be worthy to enjoy certain privileges without being perfect.

> Perhaps it is reasonable to conclude that personal measurement or judgment oftentimes may be severe and inaccurate. We may get bogged down as we try to understand and define worthiness. All of us are particularly aware of our shortcomings and weaknesses.

Therefore, it is easy for us to feel that we are unworthy of blessings we desire and that we are not as worthy to hold an office or calling as someone next door. (*Ensign*, May 1989, p. 20)

If you are uncertain regarding your worthiness, once again it is recommended that you follow Elder Ashton's counsel:

When we take it upon ourselves to pass self-judgment and simply declare "I am not worthy," we build a barrier to progress and erect blockades that prevent our moving forward. We are not being fair when we judge ourselves. A second or third opinion will always be helpful and proper. (*Ensign*, May 1989, p. 20)

In this same talk, Elder Ashton goes on to say:

I feel that one of the great myths we would do well to dispel is that we have come to earth to perfect ourselves, and nothing short of that will do. If I understand the teachings of the prophets of this dispensation correctly, we will not become perfect in this life, though we can make significant strides toward that goal. (*Ensign*, May 1989, p. 20)

Joseph Fielding Smith taught the following regarding perfection:

Salvation does not come all at once; we are commanded to be perfect even as our Father in Heaven is perfect. It will take us ages to accomplish this end, for there will be greater progress beyond the grave, and it will be there that the faithful will overcome all things, and receive all things, even the fulness of the Father's glory.

I believe the Lord meant just what he said: that we should be perfect, as our Father in Heaven is perfect. That will not come all at once, but line upon line, and precept upon precept, example upon example, and even then not as long as we live in this mortal life, for we will have to go even beyond the grave before we reach that perfection and shall be like God. (*Doctrines of Salvation*, comp. Bruce R. McConkie, 3 vols., Salt Lake City: Bookcraft, 1954-56, 2:18-19.)

A good beginning would be to read Jacob's counsel to fathers to make certain you are not guilty of any of the sins he specifies (Jacob 2, 3). Church leaders have counseled fathers to be faithful in reading the scriptures, in attending the temple when possible, in fulfilling their church assignments and, just like Jacob of old, in keeping themselves free of all forms of lasciviousness (i.e., R-rated movies, pornography).

It is a serious mistake for a father to judge himself unworthy to perform his duties as a patriarch and then do nothing about it. When this happens, a father's progress stops. Any father who considers himself unworthy is encouraged to exercise faith in the following prayer expressed by Elder Marvin J. Ashton:

> It is my hope and prayer that we will learn individually and collectively the importance of the process of becoming worthy. We are entitled to the help of others not only in assessing our worthiness but also in making the classification of "worthy" available to each of us. As we measure our worthiness, let us no longer put limitations upon ourselves. Rather, let us use those strengths and powers that are available to make us worthy to gain great heights in personal development. Thus we will reap the joy that comes to those who desire to improve and move forward with determination and effectiveness as they practice self-discipline and refuse to judge themselves as unworthy. (*Ensign*, May 1989, p. 22)

One of Satan's major ploys is to deceive people about their worthiness. In some instances he attempts to get people to excuse or minimize their shortcomings. With others, his effort is to get them to believe they cannot rise above their failings. You will be in error if you adopt either of these points of view. The gospel of Jesus Christ stresses the importance of acknowledging failings and imperfections, but at the same time the central message of the gospel is that a person can rise above them.

Desire Righteous Dominion

You will discover that as you righteously exercise the keys of the priesthood in behalf of your children on a regular basis:

> The doctrines of the priesthood shall distill upon thy soul as the dews from heaven.
>
> The Holy Ghost shall be thy constant companion, and thy scepter an unchanging scepter of righteousness and truth; and thy dominion shall be an everlasting dominion, and without compulsory means it shall flow unto thee forever and ever. (D&C 121:45-46)

Some people have the mistaken idea that any dominion in human relationships is bad, when in fact righteous dominion is a very positive relationship. God exercises righteous dominion over us, and we are blessed in the relationship. Righteous dominion of your children in this life and in the life hereafter is something you should desire with all your heart. It is the Lord's desire that your righteous dominion—not that of a bishop or even a prophet—be the greatest influence in the lives of your children.

Fruits of Success

There are some obvious milestones of your success as a patriarch (i.e., children going on missions and being married in the temple). In the writings of Mormon regarding Mosiah, the son of King Benjamin, the Lord summarizes the ultimate fruits you can expect to see as you exercise your patriarchal keys in righteousness.

Your children will keep the Lord's commandments:

> And it came to pass that king Mosiah did walk in the ways of the Lord, and did observe his judgments and his statutes, and did keep his commandments in all things whatsoever he commanded him. (Mosiah 6:6)

Your children will strive to emulate your righteous characteristics:

> And king Mosiah did cause his people that they should till the earth. And he also, himself, did till the earth, that thereby he might not become burdensome to his people, that he might do according to that which his father had done in all things. And there was no contention among all his people for the space of three years. (Mosiah 6:7)

Your children will earn the respect and esteem of righteous people:

> And they did wax strong in love towards Mosiah; yea, they did esteem him more than any other man; for they did not look upon him as a tyrant who was seeking for gain, yea, for that lucre which doth corrupt the soul; for he had not exacted riches of them, neither had he delighted in the shedding of blood; but he had established peace in the land, and he had granted unto his people that they should be delivered from all manner of bondage; therefore they did esteem him, yea, exceedingly, beyond measure. (Mosiah 29:40)

From these statements about Mosiah, it is evident that King Benjamin qualified to perform his patriarchal duties. Resolve to be equally qualified as a patriarch in your own home. As a father you will be pleased when your children are respected and held in high esteem by righteous people, especially when you know your children are living righteously and the patriarchal keys are blessing the lives of your grandchildren. As this proves the case, you can be assured you have been effective in exercising your patriarchal keys.

Help Your Children Cultivate an Abiding Faith in God

As a father you need to realize that having faith in God entails more than professing a belief in him. Your children will not enjoy all the blessings associated with membership in the church of Jesus Christ unless they have an abiding faith in God. If your children do not have a conviction that God lives, they will be prone to let situations—not revealed truth—determine their conduct. Verbal expressions of conviction are not sufficient. Your children need to understand that "without faith it is impossible to please [God]" (Hebrews 11:6).

Faith in God is the thing that will give your children the absolute assurance that, if they live righteously, God will help them cope with the challenges they will face throughout their lives. Children need to be taught that obedience is the only way they can express or demonstrate their faith in God. On one occasion President Ezra Taft Benson said, "Unless we do His teachings we do not demonstrate faith in Him." (*Come Unto Christ*, p. 132.) From the writings of Moses, we learn that faith has to be taught (see Moses 6:23). As a patriarch you can do many things to strengthen your children's faith in God.

Express Conviction

Of all the things you can do to help your children develop faith in God, the expression of conviction is the simplest. Yet, your expressions of conviction will have a profound influence on your children. Look for opportunities to express your conviction to your children in private conversations as well as in formal meetings. As a patriarch, you have the authority to hold testimony meetings in your home. Testimony meetings held at home provide an opportunity for your children to hear you express your conviction more frequently. In such meetings, not only do your children hear you testify, they can in turn express their conviction, love and appreciation.

Alma made it a practice to bear his testimony to his children:

> And I would not that ye think that I know of myself—not of the temporal but of the spiritual, not of the carnal mind but of God.
>
> Now, behold, I say unto you, if I had not been born of God I should not have known these things; but God has, by the mouth of his holy angel, made these things known unto me, not of any worthiness of myself. (Alma 36:4-5)

• • •

> Now, my son, I would not that ye should think that I know these things of myself, but it is the Spirit of God which is in me which maketh these things known unto me; for if I had not been born of God I should not have known these things. (Alma 38:6)

• • •

> For because of the word which he has imparted unto me, behold, many have been born of God, and have tasted as I have tasted, and have seen eye to eye as I have seen; therefore they do know of these things of which I have spoken, as I do know; and the knowledge which I have is of God. (Alma 36:26)

• • •

And I know that he will raise me up at the last day, to dwell with him in glory; yea, and I will praise him forever, for he has brought our fathers out of Egypt, and he has swallowed up the Egyptians in the Red Sea; and he led them by his power into the promised land; yea, and he has delivered them out of bondage and captivity from time to time. (Alma 36:28)

Lehi bore his testimony to his children:

But behold the Lord hath redeemed my soul from hell; I have beheld his glory, and I am encircled about eternally in the arms of his love. (2 Nephi 1:15)

• • •

Yea, thus prophesied Joseph: I am sure of this thing, even as I am sure of the promise of Moses; for the Lord hath said unto me, I will preserve thy seed forever. (2 Nephi 3:16)

King Benjamin bore his testimony to his children:

O my sons, I would that ye should remember that these sayings are true, and also that these records are true. And behold, also the plates of Nephi, which contain the records and the sayings of our fathers from the time they left Jerusalem until now, and they are true; and we can know of their surety because we have them before our eyes. (Mosiah 1:6)

Share Faith-Promoting Experiences

Make it a practice to look for opportunities to share faith-promoting experiences with your children. These can be experiences from your youth, mission, etc., as well as experiences involving your children. As you do this consistently while your children are growing up, you will successfully instill in your children an attitude of faith.

Lehi shared spiritual experiences with his children. The following account, written by Nephi, is based on an experience his father had shared with him:

And it came to pass as he prayed unto the Lord, there came a pillar of fire and dwelt upon a rock before him; and he saw and heard much; and because of the things which he saw and heard he did quake and tremble exceedingly.

And it came to pass that he returned to his own house at Jerusalem; and he cast himself upon his bed, being overcome with the Spirit and the things which he had seen.

And being thus overcome with the Spirit, he was carried away in a vision, even that he saw the heavens open, and he thought he saw God sitting upon his throne, surrounded with numberless concourses of angels in the attitude of singing and praising their God. (1 Nephi 1:6-8)

Another example of Lehi sharing a spiritual experience with his children is Nephi's account of his father telling his children of his vision of the Tree of Life (see 1 Nephi 8:2-25). It is interesting to note that Nephi's desire to understand the vision his father had shared with his children led to Nephi experiencing several glorious visions (see 1 Nephi 11, 12, 13, 14).

From Alma's writings we see that he shared faith-promoting experiences with his children. In his writings to his son Helaman, Alma tells him about his experience being visited by an angel and his later success as a missionary:

But behold, the Lord in his great mercy sent his angel to declare unto me that I must stop the work of destruction among his people; yea, and I have seen an angel face to face, and he spake with me, and his voice was as thunder, and it shook the whole earth.

And it came to pass that I was three days and three nights in the most bitter pain and anguish of soul; and never, until I did cry out unto the Lord Jesus Christ for mercy, did I receive a remission of my sins. But behold, I did cry unto him and I did find peace to my soul. (Alma 38:7-8) (See also Alma 36:26-27)

• • •

Yea, and from that time even until now, I have labored without ceasing, that I might bring souls unto repentance; that I might bring them to taste of the exceeding joy of which I did taste; that they might also be born of God, and be filled with the Holy Ghost.

Yea, and now behold, O my son, the Lord doth give me exceedingly great joy in the fruit of my labors;

For because of the word which he has imparted unto me, behold, many have been born of God, and have tasted as I have tasted, and have seen eye to eye as I have seen; therefore they do know of these things of which I have spoken, as I do know; and the knowledge which I have is of God.

And I have been supported under trials and troubles of every kind, yea, and in all manner of afflictions; yea, God has delivered me from prison, and from bonds, and from death; yea, and I do put my trust in him, and he will still deliver me. (Alma 36:24-27)

You will discover that as your children become aware of faith-promoting experiences associated with their family they will draw on these accounts when they give talks. When this happens, the experiences begin to live for them. As your children feel the witness of the spirit associated with faith-promoting experiences, their testimonies will be strengthened.

Help Your Children Recognize Spiritual Experiences

We are commanded to recognize the hand of the Lord in all things (see D&C 59:21). All too frequently, young people are blessed by the Lord and yet they fail to see the hand of the Lord in the situation. As a patriarch, make it a practice to help your children acknowledge the hand of the Lord in their daily experiences. A faith-promoting experience will not increase a child's faith unless it is acknowledged as such. The following verses are an account of Alma helping his son Shiblon understand one of his own spiritual experiences:

> I say unto you, my son, that I have had great joy in thee already, because of thy faithfulness and thy diligence, and thy patience and thy long-suffering among the people of the Zoramites.
>
> For I know that thou wast in bonds; yea, and I also know that thou wast stoned for the word's sake; and thou didst bear all these things with patience because the Lord was with thee; and now thou knowest that the Lord did deliver thee.
>
> And now my son, Shiblon, I would that ye should remember, that as much as ye shall put your trust in God even so much ye shall be delivered out of your trials, and your troubles, and your afflictions, and ye shall be lifted up at the last day. (Alma 38:3-5)

Lehi helped his children recognize spiritual experiences. In the following account he helped his older sons see the hand of the Lord in an experience they had had with their younger brother Nephi:

> And ye have murmured because he hath been plain unto you. Ye say that he hath used sharpness; ye say that he hath been angry with you; but behold, his sharpness was the sharpness of the power of the word of God, which was in him; and that which ye call anger was the truth, according to that which is in God, which he could not restrain, manifesting boldly concerning your iniquities.
>
> And it must needs be that the power of God must be with him, even unto his commanding you that ye must obey. But behold, it was not he, but it was the Spirit of the Lord which was in him, which opened his mouth to utterance that he could not shut it. (2 Nephi 1:26-27)

By making your children more aware of their own spiritual experiences, they will become more conscious of the workings of the spirit. When children are conscious of the workings of the spirit in their daily lives, they become much more receptive to the promptings of the Holy Ghost.

Counsel Your Children Based on Spiritual Discernment

As you live worthy of the companionship of the Holy Ghost, you can be inspired regarding your children if you prayerfully seek inspiration and then learn to trust your inner feelings. With i. spiration to guide you, you can insightfully counsel your children. Your counsel will consistently take into account a child's particular personality and disposition.

Without spiritual discernment, you will be prone to give inadequate counsel. When this happens, antagonisms can develop between you and your children. In contrast, if your counsel is based on spiritual discernment, you will be much more effective in your effort to counsel your children. If your children live righteously, they will trust that the counsel you give them comes from their Heavenly Father. As a result, their love and appreciation for God will increase.

As a patriarch, Alma counseled his children based on his spiritual discernment. The following account of Alma counseling his son Corianton was prompted by his spiritual discernment:

> Now my son, here is somewhat more I would say unto thee; for I perceive that thy mind is worried concerning the resurrection of the dead.
>
> Behold, I say unto you, that there is no resurrection—or, I would say, in other words, that this mortal does not put on immortality, this corruption does not put on incorruption—until after the coming of Christ. (Alma 40:1-2)

Alma personalized his counsel to Helaman and Shiblon:

> O, remember, my son, and learn wisdom in thy youth; yea, learn in thy youth to keep the commandments of God.
>
> Yea, and cry unto God for all thy support; yea, let all thy doings be unto the Lord, and whithersoever thou goest let it be in the Lord; yea, let thy thoughts be directed unto the Lord; yea, let the affections of thy heart be placed upon the Lord forever.

Counsel with the Lord in all thy doings, and he will direct thee for good; yea, when thou liest down at night lie down unto the Lord, that he may watch over you in your sleep; and when thou risest in the morning let thy heart be full of thanks unto God; and if ye do these things, ye shall be lifted up at the last day. (Alma 37:35-37)

• • •

And now, my son, I have told you this that ye may learn wisdom, that ye may learn of me that there is no other way or means whereby man can be saved, only in and through Christ. Behold, he is the life and the light of the world. Behold, he is the word of truth and righteousness.

And now, as ye have begun to teach the word even so I would that ye should continue to teach; and I would that ye would be diligent and temperate in all things.

See that ye are not lifted up unto pride; yea, see that ye do not boast in your own wisdom, nor of your much strength.

Use boldness, but not overbearance; and also see that ye bridle all your passions, that ye may be filled with love; see that ye refrain from idleness.

Do not pray as the Zoramites do, for ye have seen that they pray to be heard of men, and to be praised for their wisdom.

Do not say: O God, I thank thee that we are better than our brethren; but rather say: O Lord, forgive my unworthiness, and remember my brethren in mercy—yea, acknowledge your unworthiness before God at all times. (Alma 38:9-14)

Lehi also counseled his children based on spiritual discernment.

And when my father saw that the waters of the river emptied into the fountain of the Red Sea, he spake unto Laman, saying: O that thou mightest be like unto this river, continually running into the fountain of righteousness.

And he also spake unto Lemuel: O that thou mightest be like unto this valley, firm and steadfast, and immovable in keeping the commandments of the Lord!

Now this he spake because of the stiffneckedness of Laman and Lemuel; for behold they did murmur in many things against their father, because he was a visionary man, and had led them out of the land of Jerusalem, to leave the land of their inheritance, and their gold, and their silver, and their precious things, to perish in the wilderness. And this they said he had done because of the foolish imaginations of his heart. (1 Nephi 2:9-11)

Pray for spiritual discernment regarding your children daily. Discernment is a gift of the spirit, and the Lord has stipulated that we must seek the gifts of the spirit (see 1 Cor. 12:31; D&C 46:8; 1 Cor. 14:1; D&C 46:29). You will find that with the spirit of discernment to assist you, you will be much more aware of your children's moods, feelings, desires, fears, etc. You will discover that, as the spirit reveals things to your mind about your children, you will be very insightful in counseling them.

Speak to Your Children in Behalf of the Lord

A prophet has the authority to speak to all mankind in behalf of the Lord. As a patriarch you have the authority to speak to your children in behalf of the Lord. God will not become a reality to your children unless they know on a fairly regular basis that the Lord is aware of them and is inspiring people that love them in their behalf.

Alma was very bold in speaking to his children in behalf of the Lord. The following is an example:

And now the Spirit of the Lord doth say unto me: Command thy children to do good, lest they lead away the hearts of many people to destruction; there-

41

fore I command you, my son, in the fear of God, that ye refrain from your iniquities. (Alma 39:12)

Lehi spoke to his children in behalf of the Lord:

And it came to pass that I, Nephi, returned from speaking with the Lord, to the tent of my father.

And it came to pass that he spake unto me, saying: Behold I have dreamed a dream, in the which the Lord hath commanded me that thou and thy brethren shall return to Jerusalem.

For behold, Laban hath the record of the Jews and also a genealogy of my forefathers, and they are engraven upon plates of brass. (1 Nephi 3:1-3)

• • •

And now I would that ye might know, that after my father, Lehi, had made an end of prophesying concerning his seed, it came to pass that the Lord spake unto him again, saying that it was not meet for him, Lehi, that he should take his family into the wilderness alone; but that his sons should take daughters to wife, that they might raise up seed unto the Lord in the land of promise.

And it came to pass that the Lord commanded him that I, Nephi, and my brethren, should again return unto the land of Jerusalem, and bring down Ishmael and his family into the wilderness. (1 Nephi 7:1-2)

As you speak to your children in behalf of the Lord, let your children know that the Lord has confidence in them. It is very important that children hear this from their father. In the following example, Alma tells his son, Helaman, that the Lord has confidence in him:

And now remember, my son, that God has entrusted you with these things, which are sacred, which he has kept sacred, and also which he will keep and preserve for a wise purpose in him, that he may show forth his power unto future generations. (Alma 37:14)

As you consistently let your children know that the Lord is inspiring you in their behalf, they will know the Lord loves them. In addition, they will sense keenly that the Lord is aware of them. This awareness will give your children a greater resolve to resist temptation.

Make Your Children Aware of the Mercies of God

Being mindful of the mercies of God is a basic prerequisite to experiencing a witness of the spirit (see Moroni 10:3). As you help your children become aware of the mercies of God, especially those that have been extended to your immediate family and your ancestors, your children will develop an appreciation for the goodness of God. They will trust him to bless them in their trials and afflictions. Knowing this, Alma systematically made his children aware of how merciful the Lord had been to their forefathers:

> I would that ye should do as I have done, in remembering the captivity of our fathers; for they were in bondage, and none could deliver them except it was the God of Abraham, and the God of Isaac, and the God of Jacob; and he surely did deliver them in their afflictions. (Alma 36:2)
>
> • • •
>
> And I know that he will raise me up at the last day, to dwell with him in glory; yea, and I will praise him forever, for he has brought our fathers out of Egypt, and he has swallowed up the Egyptians in the Red Sea; and he led them by his power into the promised land; yea, and he has delivered them out of bondage and captivity from time to time.
>
> Yea, and he has also brought our fathers out of the land of Jerusalem; and he has also, by his everlasting power, delivered them out of bondage and captivity, from time to time even down to the present day; and I have always retained in remembrance their captivity; yea, and ye also ought to retain in remembrance, as I have done, their captivity. (Alma 36:28-29)

43

Lehi made his children aware of the mercies of God:

> And now it came to pass that after I, Nephi, had made an end of teaching my brethren, our father, Lehi, also spake many things unto them, and rehearsed unto them, how great things the Lord had done for them in bringing them out of the land of Jerusalem.
>
> And he spake unto them concerning their rebellions upon the waters, and the mercies of God in sparing their lives, that they were not swallowed up in the sea.
>
> And he also spake unto them concerning the land of promise, which they had obtained—how merciful the Lord had been in warning us that we should flee out of the land of Jerusalem.
>
> For, behold, said he, I have seen a vision, in which I know that Jerusalem is destroyed; and had we remained in Jerusalem we should also have perished.
>
> But, said he, notwithstanding our afflictions, we have obtained a land of promise, a land which is choice above all other lands; a land which the Lord God hath covenanted with me should be a land for the inheritance of my seed. Yea, the Lord hath covenanted this land unto me, and to my children forever, and also all those who should be led out of other countries by the hand of the Lord. (2 Nephi 1:1-5)

As your children are consistently made aware of the mercies of God, they will develop a spirit of gratitude for their many blessings. You will find that if your children feel a spirit of gratitude they will be much more disposed to bear their testimonies.

President Ezra Taft Benson has admonished parents to teach their children to express gratitude in their prayers:

> The Prophet Joseph is reported to have said at one time that one of the greatest sins for which the Latter-day Saints would be guilty would be the sin of

ingratitude. I presume most of us have not thought of that as a serious sin. There is a great tendency for us in our prayers—in our pleadings with the Lord—to ask for additional blessings. Sometimes I feel we need to devote more of our prayers to expressions of gratitude and thanksgiving for blessings already received. Of course we need the daily blessings of the Lord. But if we sin in the matter of prayer, I think it is in our lack of the expressions of thanksgiving for daily blessings. (*Teachings of Ezra Taft Benson*, p. 363)

• • •

God help us to be grateful for our blessings, never to be guilty of the sin of ingratitude, and to instill this same gratitude into the lives of our children. Someone has said that an ungrateful man is like a hog under a tree eating apples and never looking up to see where they come from. And the Lord has said, "And he who receiveth all things with thankfulness shall be made glorious; and the things of this earth shall be added unto him, even an hundred fold, yea, more" (D&C 78:19). This great principle of gratitude, made a daily part of our lives and our prayers, can lift and bless us as individuals, as members of the Church, and as parents and families. (*Teachings of Ezra Taft Benson*, p. 364)

Quote From the Scriptures

As you make it a practice to quote or read from the scriptures when you instruct your children, they will learn many lessons of life and will see the results of wickedness and righteousness in the lives of others. President Spencer W. Kimball spoke on the importance of children being conversant with the scriptures. The following are excerpts from his writings:

Scripture study is a family responsibility. Scripture study as individuals and as a family is most fundamental to learning the gospel. Daily reading of the scriptures and discussing them together has long been suggested as a powerful tool against ignorance and the temptations of Satan. This practice will produce great happiness and will help family members love the Lord and his goodness. . . . Home is where we become experts and scholars in gospel righteousness. (*Teachings of Spencer W. Kimball*, p. 129)

• • •

Youth need literacy in scriptures. Gospel, doctrine, or organization illiteracy should never be found among our youth. Proper scriptures can be learned well and permanently by children; doctrines can be taught and absorbed by youth. (*Teachings of Spencer W. Kimball*, pp. 129-130)

• • •

Scriptures illustrate good and evil. We learn the lessons of life more readily and surely if we see the results of wickedness and righteousness in the lives of others. To know the patriarchs and prophets of ages past and their faithfulness under stress and temptation and persecution strengthens the resolves of youth. (*Teachings of Spencer W. Kimball*, pp. 131-132)

• • •

Our children may learn the lessons of life through the perseverance and personal strength of Nephi; the godliness of the three Nephites; the faith of Abraham; the power of Moses; the deception and perfidy of Ananias; the courage even to death of the unresisting Ammonites; the unassailable faith of the Lamanite mothers transmitted down through their sons, so powerful that it saved Helaman's striplings. Not a single one came to his death in that war. (*Teachings of Spencer W. Kimball*, pp. 132-133)

Lehi quoted the scriptures extensively in his conversations with his children:

And now, Joseph, my last-born, whom I have brought out of the wilderness of mine afflictions, may the Lord bless thee forever, for thy seed shall not utterly be destroyed.

For behold, thou art the fruit of my loins; and I am a descendant of Joseph who was carried captive into Egypt. And great were the covenants of the Lord which he made unto Joseph.

Wherefore, Joseph truly saw our day. And he obtained a promise of the Lord, that out of the fruit of his loins the Lord God would raise up a righteous branch unto the house of Israel; not the Messiah, but a branch which was to be broken off, nevertheless, to be remembered in the covenants of the Lord that the Messiah should be made manifest unto them in the latter days, in the spirit of power, unto the bringing of them out of darkness unto light—yea, out of hidden darkness and out of captivity unto freedom.

For Joseph truly testified, saying: A seer shall the Lord my God raise up, who shall be a choice seer unto the fruit of my loins.

Yea, Joseph truly said: Thus saith the Lord unto me: A choice seer will I raise up out of the fruit of thy loins; and he shall be esteemed highly among the fruit of thy loins. And unto him will I give command-ment that he shall do a work for the fruit of thy loins, his brethren, which shall be of great worth unto them, even to the bringing of them to the knowledge of the covenants which I have made with thy fathers.

And I will give unto him a commandment that he shall do none other work, save the work which I shall command him. And I will make him great in mine eyes; for he shall do my work.

And he shall be great like unto Moses, whom I have said I would raise up unto you, to deliver my people, O house of Israel.

And Moses will I raise up, to deliver thy people out of the land of Egypt.

But a seer will I raise up out of the fruit of thy loins; and unto him will I give power to bring forth my word unto the seed of thy loins—and not to the bringing forth my word only, saith the Lord, but to the convincing them of my word, which shall have already gone forth among them.

Wherefore, the fruit of thy loins shall write; and the fruit of the loins of Judah shall write; and that which shall be written by the fruit of thy loins, and also that which shall be written by the fruit of the loins of Judah, shall grow together, unto the confounding of false doctrines and laying down of contentions, and establishing peace among the fruit of thy loins, and bringing them to the knowledge of my covenants, saith the Lord.

And out of weakness he shall be made strong, in that day when my work shall commence among all my people, unto the restoring thee, O house of Israel, saith the Lord.

And thus prophesied Joseph, saying: Behold, that seer will the Lord bless; and they that seek to destroy him shall be confounded; for this promise, which I have obtained of the Lord, of the fruit of my loins, shall be fulfilled. Behold, I am sure of the fulfilling of this promise;

And his name shall be called after me; and it shall be after the name of his father. And he shall be like unto me; for the thing, which the Lord shall bring forth by his hand, by the power of the Lord shall bring my people unto salvation.

Yea, thus prophesied Joseph: I am sure of this thing, even as I am sure of the promise of Moses; for the Lord hath said unto me, I will preserve thy seed forever.

And the Lord hath said: I will raise up a Moses; and I will give power unto him in a rod; and I will give judgment unto him in writing. Yet I will not loose his tongue, that he shall speak much, for I will not make him mighty in speaking. But I will write unto him my law, by the finger of mine own hand; and I will make a spokesman for him.

And the Lord said unto me also; I will raise up unto the fruit of thy loins; and I will make for him a spokesman. And I, behold, I will give unto him that he shall write the writing of the fruit of thy loins, unto the fruit of thy loins; and the spokesman of thy loins shall declare it.

And the words which he shall write shall be the words which are expedient in my wisdom should go forth unto the fruit of thy loins. And it shall be as if the fruit of thy loins had cried unto them from the dust; for I know their faith.

And they shall cry from the dust; yea, even repentance unto their brethren, even after many generations have gone by them. And it shall come to pass that their cry shall go, even according to the simpleness of their words.

Because of their faith their words shall proceed forth out of my mouth unto their brethren who are the fruit of thy loins; and the weakness of their words will I make strong in their faith, unto the remembering of my covenant which I made unto thy fathers.

And now, behold, my son Joseph, after this manner did my father of old prophesy. (2 Nephi 3:3-22)

From the writings of Nephi we learn why it is important to read the scriptures to your children:

Now it came to pass that I, Nephi, did read many things to them, which were engraven upon the plates of brass, that they might know concerning the doings of the Lord in other lands, among people of old.

And I did read many things unto them which were written in the book of Moses; but that I might more fully persuade them to believe in the Lord their Redeemer I did read unto them that which was written by the prophet Isaiah; for I did liken all scriptures unto us, that it might be for our profit and learning. (1 Nephi 19:22-23)

By design, the scriptures portray every weakness and strength of man, the rewards and the punishments for righteousness and unrighteousness. By exposing your children to the scriptures, they will learn how the Lord expects them to live.

Teach Your Children That the Lord Always Fulfills His Promises

Satan would like your children to believe the Lord is whimsical in whether or not he blesses people. It is very important that your children have a firm conviction that the Lord always fulfills his promises and, as a patriarch, you play a major role in helping your children develop this conviction. The following verses are an example of Alma fulfilling this responsibility as a patriarch:

> But if ye keep the commandments of God, and do with these things which are sacred according to that which the Lord doth command you, (for you must appeal unto the Lord for all things whatsoever ye must do with them) behold, no power of earth or hell can take them from you, for God is powerful to the fulfilling of all his words.
>
> For he will fulfil all his promises which he shall make unto you, for he has fulfilled his promises which he has made unto our fathers. (Alma 37:16-17)

Look for opportunities to talk about experiences you have had which illustrate the Lord fulfilling his promises (i.e., special blessings received as a result of paying a faithful tithe). Unless you fulfil this responsibility as a patriarch to your children, you run the risk that they will believe Satan's lie that God is whimsical and does not fulfil his promises.

Your Efforts as a Patriarch Will Pay Dividends

As you successfully help your children develop an absolute faith in their Heavenly Father, they will trust him to sustain them in all of their righteous endeavors. With such faith they will be much more inclined to remain faithful in their youth, as missionaries, and as adults. With faith in God guiding them, your children will be much less self-centered and will be disposed to put the welfare of others before their own. You will discover that God will consistently work through them to bless others. Seeing your children perform acts of kindness and generosity, with no thought of recognition for themselves, will be a tremendous source of joy to you. Such acts will give you the absolute assurance that your children love the Lord, and things will generally go well for them.

5

Strengthen
Your Children

As a patriarch you should learn from the example of your Heavenly Father. Everything God does in his dealings with you is designed to strengthen and assist you in your mortal endeavors. You need to emulate him in your dealings with your children. One of your primary objectives should be to "nourish [your children] with things pertaining to righteousness" (Mosiah 23:18). A careful study of the lives of Book of Mormon fathers reveals a number of things you can do to strengthen your children.

Bless Your Children

Very basic keys of the priesthood associated with your patriarchal authority are the power and authority to bless members of your family as the spirit directs you. Many situations warrant you giving your children a special blessing; a few examples would be a child suffering stress, a child desiring guidance in making an important decision, or a child desiring to overcome a personal problem. It is appropriate for you to offer to give your children a special blessing as well as for them to request a blessing from you.

You will find that as you are reflective and prayerful, the Lord will reveal things to your mind he feels should be expressed in blessings. Also, you have the right to desire blessings for your children. If blessings you desire to pronounce are in the interest of your children, the Lord will give you confirmation that they can be pronounced. It is your responsibility to live worthy to discern the promptings of the spirit in blessing your children. You need to trust your authority to bless your children and your ability to receive inspiration to guide you in blessing them. Once you pronounce blessings, it is important that you exercise faith that blessings you pronounce in behalf of members of your family will be realized.

By virtue of his authority as a patriarch, Alma blessed his children:

> And may the Lord bless your soul, and receive you at the last day into his kingdom, to sit down in peace. Now go, my son, and teach the word unto this people. Be sober. My son, farewell. (Alma 38:15)

• • •

> And now, O my son, ye are called of God to preach the word unto this people. And now, my son, go thy way, declare the word with truth and soberness, that thou mayest bring souls unto repentance, that the great plan of mercy may have claim upon them. And may God grant unto you even according to my words. Amen. (Alma 42:31)

On various occasions Lehi blessed his children:

> Wherefore, thy soul shall be blessed, and thou shalt dwell safely with thy brother, Nephi; and thy days shall be spent in the service of thy God. Wherefore, I know that thou art redeemed, because of the righteousness of thy Redeemer; for thou hast beheld that in the fulness of time he cometh to bring salvation unto man. (2 Nephi 2:3)

• • •

And may the Lord consecrate also unto thee this land, which is a most precious land, for thine inheritance and the inheritance of thy seed with thy brethren, for thy security forever, if it so be that ye shall keep the commandments of the Holy One of Israel. (2 Nephi 3:2, 25)

Exercising your rightful authority to bless your children is something you should do frequently. Such blessings can be pronounced in family prayers as well as in conjunction with priesthood ordinances or special blessings. The following remarks by Elder Gardner H. Russell point out some of the positive things that occur when you exercise your right to bless your children:

Fathers everywhere, consider the gift of love you can give your children when you are worthy and you lay your hands upon their heads to pronounce inspired father's blessings as the family patriarch. They will feel a continuing outpouring of your love, which will keep them close to you and to the Lord. You will not have to "seek them out" later. (*Ensign*, Nov. 1986, p. 27)

In addition to blessing your children when you pray, etc., as patriarch you should give them a father's blessing when they will be leaving home for some period of time.

It is the right of every father and his duty as patriarch of his own family to give a father's blessing to his children, and it is our hope that every father will give a sacred blessing to each of his children, especially as they are leaving home to go to school or on missions or to be married, which blessing should then be noted in the individual's private journal. (President Spencer W. Kimball, *Ensign*, Nov. 1977, p. 4)

Prepare Your Children to Receive Their Patriarchal Blessings

There is no specified age for receiving a patriarchal blessing. Let the spirit guide you in suggesting to your children when they should receive their blessings. As the patriarch in your home, concern yourself with your children's preparation to receive their blessings as well as when they will profit most from their patriarchal blessings.

Speaking of patriarchal blessings President Spencer W. Kimball said, "It is a blessing for which you people should be adequately prepared, morally, mentally and spiritually" (*Teachings of Spencer W. Kimball*, p. 505). He said that fathers should encourage their children to prepare themselves to receive their blessings, but should never urge or force their children to receive their patriarchal blessings.

If you make it a practice to talk about the influence of your own blessing in your life over the years, your children will come to understand the various ways a patriarchal blessing will assist them.

In talking to your children about patriarchal blessings, give them some idea of what their blessing will address.

> In each blessing, the patriarch will declare, under inspiration, the literal blood lineage of the person to be blessed and then, as moved upon by the Spirit, make a statement as to possibilities and the special spiritual gifts, cautions, instructions, admonitions, and warnings as the patriarch may be prompted to give. . . .
>
> Patriarchal blessings are revelations to the recipients—a white line down the middle of the road to protect, inspire, motivate toward activity and righteousness. . . .
>
> An inspired patriarchal blessing could light the way and lead the recipient on a path to fulfillment. It could lead him to become a new man and to have in his body a new heart. (*Teachings of Spencer W. Kimball*, p. 505)

Being aware of the types of things that are expressed in patriarchal blessings will also help your children understand and interpret their blessings.

When one of your children decides to obtain his or her blessing, you should encourage them to approach the blessing very conscientiously. Your child may wish to fast in anticipation of the receipt of the blessing. But most importantly, your child should pray that the Lord will speak to the patriarch in his or her behalf. The child's desire should be that the blessings the Lord desires pronounced, will be pronounced.

Once your children receive their patriarchal blessings, they need to be taught that the blessings pronounced therein are conditional. On various occasions read the following statement to your children:

> *Patriarchal blessing is conditional prophecy.* The patriarch is a prophet entitled to the revelations of the Lord to each individual on whose head he places his hands. He may indicate the lineage of the individual, but he may also pour out blessings that are prophetic to the individual for his life. We hope the people of this land will avail themselves of this great blessing. The blessings which he gives are conditional. They are promised, as are most other blessings that the Lord has promised to people, contingent upon their worthiness and fulfilling the obligations. There is no guarantee that the blessings will be fulfilled unless the individual subscribes to the program, but I bear my testimony to you that none of the blessings he pronounces will fail if the participant of the blessing fully subscribes. (*Teachings of Spencer W. Kimball*, p. 504)

Attempt to help your children appreciate the guidance their patriarchal blessings will provide them. Unless you perform your role, there is the danger that your children will lose sight of their blessings. If this happens, one of the most fundamental purposes for a patriarchal blessing is lost. Commenting on this function of a blessing, President Spencer W. Kimball made the following remark:

> *Patriarchal blessing offers guidance.* The patriarchal blessing may not be necessary for salvation, but is a

guidepost; a white line down the middle of the road; a series of stakes around the mountain pass with reflector buttons in them so that whenever needed in the darkness and in the storm, they are available. The blessing can be reread like the reflectors that come up as the car approaches them on the turns. (*Teachings of Spencer W. Kimball*, p. 505)

It is not your role as a father to interpret your children's patriarchal blessings. However, you may want to read them occasionally with your children's consent, and with the intent to help ensure they do not lose sight of the blessings pronounced.

Teach Your Children the Gospel When You Perform Priesthood Ordinances

When you perform priesthood ordinances in behalf of your children (i.e., confirmations, ordinations, father's blessings), let the spirit guide you in teaching them various aspects of the gospel. An example of a father teaching his children the gospel while giving a blessing is Lehi blessing his son Jacob. In this blessing, Lehi explained why it was necessary that there be opposition in all things (see 2 Nephi 2:1-30). In the first part of the blessing, Lehi compliments Jacob, then promises him that he will be blessed and tells him he will dwell safely with his brother Nephi. He then proceeds to tell Jacob that he has been redeemed. Lehi spends the rest of the blessing teaching Jacob why we need to have opposition in our lives.

Openly Express Your Feelings and Desires to Your Children

As a patriarch you should make it a practice to openly express your feelings to your children on a regular basis, especially your love and desires. You should continue expressing your feelings and desires to your children even when they are older. In some respects, older children need to hear you express your feelings and desires more than younger children. Lehi provides an excellent example as he continued to express his feelings and his desires to his children even after they were married:

> O my sons, that these things might not come upon you, but that ye might be a choice and a favored people of the Lord. But behold, his will be done; for his ways are righteousness forever. (2 Nephi 1:19)

• • •

> And now that my soul might have joy in you, and that my heart might leave this world with gladness because of you, that I might not be brought down with grief and sorrow to the grave, arise from the dust, my sons, and be men, and be determined in one mind and in one heart, united in all things, that ye may not come down into captivity;
>
> That ye may not be cursed with a sore cursing; and also, that ye may not incur the displeasure of a just God upon you, unto the destruction, yea, the eternal destruction of both soul and body.
>
> Awake, my sons; put on the armor of righteousness. Shake off the chains with which ye are bound, and come forth out of obscurity, and arise from the dust.
>
> Rebel no more against your brother, whose views have been glorious, and who hath kept the commandments from the time that we left Jerusalem; and who hath been an instrument in the hands of God, in bringing us forth into the land of promise; for were it not for him, we must have perished with hunger in the wilderness; nevertheless, ye sought to take away his life; yea, and he hath suffered much sorrow because of you.
>
> And I exceedingly fear and tremble because of you, lest he shall suffer again; for behold, ye have accused him that he sought power and authority over you; but I know that he hath not sought for power nor authority over you, but he hath sought the glory of God, and your own eternal welfare. (2 Nephi 1:21-25)

> And now, my sons, I would that ye should look to the great Mediator, and hearken unto his great commandments; and be faithful unto his words, and choose eternal life, according to the will of his Holy Spirit;
>
> And not choose eternal death, according to the will of the flesh and the evil which is therein, which giveth the spirit of the devil power to captivate, to bring you down to hell, that he may reign over you in his own kingdom. (2 Nephi 2:28-29)

• • •

> And it came to pass after my father, Lehi, had spoken unto all his household, according to the feelings of his heart and the Spirit of the Lord which was in him, he waxed old. And it came to pass that he died, and was buried. (2 Nephi 4:12)

The expression of feelings to your children, along with an appropriate hug, will strengthen your relationship with them. If you consistently express your righteous desires in behalf of your children, such expressions will also help bond your relationship with them. When there is a death in the family, parents and children often express regret that they didn't express their love to one another more frequently. Resolve to prevent this common remorse.

Compliment Your Children

In our present society, children receive a lot of criticism from adults and their peers. If a father fails in his responsibility to compliment his children on a regular basis, there is a danger the children will develop low self-esteem. Children with low self-esteem are much more susceptible to drugs and other temptations. Look for reasons to praise your children. Make it a practice to encourage your children in all their constructive endeavors, and to let them know when their thoughts, words, and actions are pleasing to the Lord.

Alma set an example for all fathers in complimenting his son Shiblon:

> And now, my son, I trust that I shall have great joy in you, because of your steadiness and your faithfulness unto God; for as you have commenced in your youth to look to the Lord your God, even so I hope that you will continue in keeping his commandments; for blessed is he that endureth to the end.
>
> I say unto you, my son, that I have had great joy in thee already, because of thy faithfulness and thy diligence, and thy patience and thy long-suffering among the people of the Zoramites. (Alma 38:2-3)

Lehi complimented his children:

> And now, Jacob, I speak unto you: Thou art my first-born in the days of my tribulation in the wilderness. And behold, in thy childhood thou hast suffered afflictions and much sorrow, because of the rudeness of thy brethren.
>
> Nevertheless, Jacob, my first-born in the wilderness, thou knowest the greatness of God; and he shall consecrate thine afflictions for thy gain. (2 Nephi 2:1-2)

From the following comment of Nephi, it is very clear that his father had let him know he was pleased with him:

> And it came to pass that when my father had heard these words he was exceedingly glad, for he knew that I had been blessed of the Lord. (1 Nephi 3:8)

When God spoke from heaven at Jesus' baptism, He complimented His son by saying, "This is my beloved son, in whom I am well pleased." (Matthew 3:17)

Strive to compliment your children at least five times as frequently as you correct them. If you are consistent in this practice, your children will feel good about themselves.

Prophesy Regarding Your Family

As a patriarch you are entitled to prophesy regarding your family, whether collectively or individually. Such prophecies can deal with any aspect of their lives (i.e., school, social life), as well as church callings and responsibilities. In letters, blessings, or conversations you can make prophetic statements. For example, if you had a son on a mission who had just been assigned to work in a difficult area, and if the Lord revealed to you that your son would be blessed in his new assignment, in a letter you could say "I am confident the Lord will prepare the way for you to have success if you are diligent in your labors" or "The Lord has given me to know that you are going to have success in your new area."

The following are examples of Lehi prophesying regarding his family:

> But behold, I have obtained a land of promise, in the which things I do rejoice; yea, and I know that the Lord will deliver my sons out of the hands of Laban, and bring them down again unto us in the wilderness. (1 Nephi 5:5)

> And now when my father saw all these things, he was filled with the Spirit, and began to prophesy concerning his seed—

> That these plates of brass should go forth unto all nations, kindreds, tongues, and people who were of his seed.

> Wherefore, he said that these plates of brass should never perish; neither should they be dimmed any more by time. And he prophesied many things concerning his seed. (1 Nephi 5:17-19)

Many times over the years, your prophecies regarding your children will be the thing that gives them the determination to endure in righteousness when they face adversity.

The Importance of High Self-Esteem

If you consistently fail to do things as a patriarch that strengthen your children, they may develop low self-esteem. Children with low self-esteem are very susceptible to the enticements of Satan. Another negative consequence of low self-esteem is despair. When children succumb to despair, they become very unhappy, and in some instances even suicidal.

If you as a patriarch will assume the responsibility to nourish your children in righteousness, they will have much greater resolve to resist temptation. Also, they will feel good about themselves and find meaning in life. When children are in this frame of mind, they learn to appreciate the Lord's pronouncement, "Men are that they might have joy" (2 Nephi 2:25).

As children are successful in finding meaning in life, they can make clear distinctions between activities that are fun but self-serving and those that bring joy and fulfillment. This is one of the most important lessons your children can learn as they are growing up. This lesson will safeguard your children against pride.

President Ezra Taft Benson made the following comment regarding the relationship between selfishness and pride:

> Pride is characterized by "what do I want out of life" rather than by "what would God have me do with my life." It is self will as opposed to God's will. (A Witness and a Warning, p. 78)

6

Inspire Your Children to Live Righteously

Unfortunately, some fathers have the mistaken idea that once they have taught their children what is "right" and what is "wrong," they have performed their duty as parents. Helping children desire to do what is right is much more important than teaching them the difference between right and wrong. In the following verses we see Helaman attempting to instill in his children a desire to live righteously:

> Behold, my sons, I desire that ye should remember to keep the commandments of God; and I would that ye should declare unto the people these words. Behold, I have given unto you the names of our first parents who came out of the land of Jerusalem; and this I have done that when you remember your names ye may remember them; and when ye remember them ye may remember their works; and when ye remember their works ye may know how that it is said, and also written, that they were good.

> And now my sons, behold I have somewhat more to desire of you, which desire is, that ye may not do these things that ye may boast, but that ye may do these things to lay up for yourselves a treasure in

> heaven, yea, which is eternal, and which fadeth not away; yea, that ye may have that precious gift of eternal life, which we have reason to suppose hath been given to our fathers. (Helaman 5:6,8)

As a father, systematically do things that will inspire your children to keep the commandments. Once again the scriptures, especially the Book of Mormon, offer insights and ideas to assist you in being an effective patriarch in this regard.

Promise Your Children They Will Be Blessed As They Live Righteously

As a patriarch, teach your children systematically the following basic tenet of the gospel of Jesus Christ:

> There is a law, irrevocably decreed in heaven before the foundations of this world, upon which all blessings are predicated—
>
> And when we obtain any blessing from God, it is by obedience to that law upon which it is predicated. (D&C 130:20-21)
>
> I, the Lord, am bound when ye do what I say; but when ye do not what I say, ye have no promise. (D&C 82:10)

Once your children have a conviction that the receipt of blessings is governed by eternal laws, they will have an unwavering faith that the Lord will stand by them and assist them as long as they are righteous.

Young women who do not come to this conviction will be prone to doubt they will be blessed with the opportunity to be married in the temple, even if they live righteously. If young women doubt that righteous young men will be attracted to them even if they live righteously they will be more susceptible to moral transgressions.

Young men who do not come to the conviction that the Lord will bless them if they live righteously will be prone to doubt their ability to earn enough money to adequately support a family. When this happens there is a danger young men will be reluctant to accept the responsibility of marriage and parenthood. Then, if they do, they may fear that they will not be able to afford a house, etc. unless their wives work. Doubting their ability to adequately provide for their families is one of the greatest temptations young men face.

Lehi repeatedly promised his children blessings if they would keep the Lord's commandments:

> And he hath said that: Inasmuch as ye shall keep my commandments ye shall prosper in the land; but inasmuch as ye will not keep my commandments ye shall be cut off from my presence. (2 Nephi 1:20)

• • •

> Wherefore, if ye shall keep the commandments of the Lord, the Lord hath consecrated this land for the security of thy seed with the seed of my son. (2 Nephi 1:32)

• • •

> And may the Lord consecrate also unto thee this land, which is a most precious land, for thine inheritance and the inheritance of thy seed with thy brethren, for thy security forever, if it so be that ye shall keep the commandments of the Holy One of Israel. (2 Nephi 3:2)

• • •

> For the Lord God hath said that: Inasmuch as ye shall keep my commandments ye shall prosper in the land; and inasmuch as ye will not keep my commandments ye shall be cut off from my presence. (2 Nephi 4:4)

Alma promised his children blessings if they would live righteously. The following verses are a few examples:

> My son, give ear to my words; for I swear unto you, that inasmuch as ye shall keep the commandments of God ye shall prosper in the land. (Alma 36:1)

• • •

And now, O my son Helaman, behold, thou art in thy youth, and therefore, I beseech of thee that thou wilt hear my words and learn of me; for I do know that whosoever shall put their trust in God shall be supported in their trials, and their troubles, and their afflictions, and shall be lifted up at the last day. (Alma 36:3)

• • •

My son, give ear to my words, for I say unto you, even as I said unto Helaman, that inasmuch as ye shall keep the commandments of God ye shall prosper in the land. (Alma 38:1)

• • •

And now my son, Shiblon, I would that ye should remember, that as much as ye shall put your trust in God even so much ye shall be delivered out of your trials, and your troubles, and your afflictions, and ye shall be lifted up at the last day. (Alma 38:5)

Consistent with the example of other righteous fathers in the Book of Mormon, King Benjamin promised his children they would prosper if they kept the Lord's commandments (see Mosiah 1:7).

Promise your children specific blessings as they keep certain commandments. For example, a father can promise his daughter specific blessings if she complies with church policy not to date before she turns sixteen. To do this, you need to be acquainted with the various promises the Lord has specified in the scriptures. The following are examples:

Cease to be idle; cease to be unclean; cease to find fault one with another; cease to sleep longer than is needful; retire to thy bed early, that ye may not be weary; arise early, that your bodies and your minds may be invigorated. (D&C 88:124)

• • •

If thou shalt ask, thou shalt receive revelation upon revelation, knowledge upon knowledge, that thou mayest know the mysteries and peaceable things—that which bringeth joy, that which bringeth life eternal. (D&C 42:61)

• • •

Yea, come unto Christ, and be perfected in him, and deny yourselves of all ungodliness; and if ye shall deny yourselves of all ungodliness and love God with all your might, mind and strength, then is his grace sufficient for you, that by his grace ye may be perfect in Christ; and if by the grace of God ye are perfect in Christ, ye can in nowise deny the power of God. (Moroni 10:32)

• • •

Bring ye all the tithes into the storehouse, that there may be meat in my house; and prove me now herewith, saith the Lord of Hosts, if I will not open you the windows of heaven, and pour you out a blessing that there shall not be room enough to receive it.

And I will rebuke the devourer for your sakes, and he shall not destroy the fruits of your ground; neither shall your vine cast her fruit before the time in the fields, saith the Lord of Hosts. (3 Nephi 24:10-11)

• • •

Honour thy father and thy mother, as the Lord thy God hath commanded thee; that thy days may be prolonged, and that it may go well with thee, in the land which the Lord thy God giveth thee. (Deut. 5:16)

• • •

And if men come unto me I will show unto them their weakness. I give unto men weakness that they may be humble; and my grace is sufficient for all men that humble themselves before me; for if they humble themselves before me, and have faith in me, then will I make weak things become strong unto them. (Ether 12:27)

As you promise your children specific blessings predicated on righteous living, they will come to a conviction that the Lord is bound when they keep his commandments (see D&C 82:10). In the course of time, their desire to live righteously will be motivated by a love of God, not the receipt of blessings. Once they are in this frame of mind, they will be blessed even more abundantly by the Lord.

Teach Children That Happiness is Found in Righteous Living

Satan wants children to believe that righteous living will not bring joy and fulfillment. If children reject the basic truth that righteousness leads to happiness, they will become very susceptible to temptation. As a father, you have the responsibility to instill in your children the knowledge that sin results in unhappiness, and that true happiness is attained only through righteous living (see Alma 41:10). In addition, children need to understand that those who are happy in this life will be happy in the hereafter. Conversely, those who as a result of sin are unhappy now will be unhappy in the eternities (see Mormon 9:14).

Strive to follow King Benjamin's example by helping your children realize that as they live righteously, they will be happy. Discuss the following verse with your children:

> And moreover, I would desire that ye should consider on the blessed and happy state of those that keep the commandments of God. For behold, they are blessed in all things, both temporal and spiritual; and if they hold out faithful to the end they are received into heaven, that thereby they may dwell with God in a state of neverending happiness. O remember that these things are true; for the Lord God hath spoken it. (Mosiah 2:41)

Do everything in your power to help your children realize that Satan is a master of deceit. He will go to great lengths to get your children to believe they can be happy in sin. President Benson has spoken out regarding Satan's effort to deceive us about sin and happiness:

> One of Satan's most frequently used deceptions is the notion that the commandments of God are meant to restrict freedom and limit happiness. Young people especially sometimes feel that the standards of the Lord are like fences and chains, blocking them from those activities that seem most enjoyable in life. But exactly the opposite is true. The gospel plan is the plan by which men are brought to a fulness of joy. The gospel principles are the steps and guidelines which will help us find true happiness and joy. (*Teachings of Ezra Taft Benson*, p. 356)

In our present society many sins are glamorized; the impression is that the people who sin have the most fun. Use the Book of Mormon to help your children realize that those who sin "have joy in their works for a season, [but] by and by the end cometh, and they are hewn down and cast into the fire, from whence there is no return" (3 Nephi 27:11).

Help Your Children See Their Great Potential As They Live Righteously

One of the major ploys of the adversary is to get young people to feel inadequate. As you help your children develop faith in things they can accomplish when living righteously, they will not be susceptible to feelings of inadequacy. They will develop confidence in their ability to accomplish constructive goals and desires.

Alma, with great insight, helped his children realize more fully their great potential when they lived righteously. The following are two examples:

> And now, my son, I trust that I shall have great joy in you, because of your steadiness and your faithfulness unto God; for as you have commenced in your youth to look to the Lord your God, even so I hope that you will continue in keeping his commandments; for blessed is he that endureth to the end. (Alma 38:2)

71

• • •

> And now, O my son, ye are called of God to preach the word unto this people. And now, my son, go thy way, declare the word with truth and soberness, that thou mayest bring souls unto repentance, that the great plan of mercy may have claim upon them. And may God grant unto you even according to my words. Amen. (Alma 42:31)

Once your children receive their patriarchal blessings, you should suggest they read them on a fairly regular basis. Patriarchal blessings will help children see their potential in righteousness.

Command Your Children in a Spirit of Love

As a patriarch, you have the authority to command your children to strive for righteous and to do constructive things. There are times to counsel and encourage children, but there are also times when you should command them, in the spirit of love as you are prompted by the Holy Ghost, to do specific things.

Alma was forthright in commanding his children to do specific things:

> And now, my son Helaman, I command you that ye take the records which have been entrusted with me;
>
> And I also command you that ye keep a record of this people, according as I have done, upon the plates of Nephi, and keep all these things sacred which I have kept, even as I have kept them; for it is for a wise purpose that they are kept. (Alma 37:1-2)

• • •

> And now, my son, I command you that ye retain all their oaths, and their covenants, and their agreements in their secret abominations; yea, and all their signs and their wonders ye shall keep from this people, that they know them not, lest peradventure they should fall into darkness also and be destroyed. (Alma 37:27)

• • •

> And I command you to take it upon you to counsel
> with your elder brothers in your undertakings; for
> behold, thou art in thy youth, and ye stand in need to
> be nourished by your brothers. And give heed to their
> counsel. (Alma 39:10)

As a patriarch, you need to command your older as well as
your younger children. In some instances, you may have to
command older children more than younger children. The
situation should be the determinant, not the age of your children.

Warn Your Children About the Consequences of Unrighteousness

Some children minimize the consequences of sin. Sin in
and of itself is destructive, but the negative consequences
compound dramatically if we excuse or minimize our sins.
This is why Satan works so hard to deceive young people
about the seriousness of their sins. It is very important that
you help your children realize the full consequences of
unrighteousness. If a father fails in this responsibility and his
children sin in ignorance, the sins will be on the head of the
father (see D&C 68:25).

You should follow Alma's example in warning your children about the consequences of unrighteousness, as in the following verses:

> And now, O my son Helaman, behold, thou art in
> thy youth, and therefore, I beseech of thee that thou
> wilt hear my words and learn of me; for I do know
> that whosoever shall put their trust in God shall be
> supported in their trials, and their troubles, and their
> afflictions, and shall be lifted up at the last day.
> (Alma 36:3)

• • •

> O remember, remember, my son Helaman, how strict
> are the commandments of God. And he said: If ye

73

will keep my commandments ye shall prosper in the land—but if ye keep not his commandments ye shall be cut off from his presence. (Alma 37:13)

• • •

And now behold, I tell you by the spirit of prophecy, that if ye transgress the commandments of God, behold, these things which are sacred shall be taken away from you by the power of God, and ye shall be delivered up unto Satan, that he may sift you as chaff before the wind. (Alma 37:15)

Lehi warned his children of the consequences of sin:

And I desire that ye should remember to observe the statutes and the judgments of the Lord; behold, this hath been the anxiety of my soul from the beginning.

My heart hath been weighed down with sorrow from time to time, for I have feared, lest for the hardness of your hearts the Lord your God should come out in the fulness of his wrath upon you, that ye be cut off and destroyed forever;

Or, that a cursing should come upon you for the space of many generations; and ye are visited by sword, and by famine, and are hated, and are led according to the will and captivity of the devil. (2 Nephi 1:16-18)

Make your children aware of the popular lies Satan reveals about sin:

And there shall also be many which shall say: Eat, drink, and be merry; nevertheless, fear God—he will justify in committing a little sin; yea, lie a little, take the advantage of one because of his words, dig a pit for thy neighbor; there is no harm in this; and do all these things, for tomorrow we die; and if it so be that we are guilty, God will beat us with a few stripes, and at last we shall be saved in the kingdom of God. (2 Nephi 28:8)

• • •

> Yea, it shall come in a day when there shall be churches built up that shall say: Come unto me, and for your money you shall be forgiven of your sins. (Mormon 8:32)

• • •

> Yea, he saith unto them: Deceive and lie in wait to catch, that ye may destroy; behold this is no harm. And thus he flattereth them, and telleth them that it is no sin to lie that they may catch a man in a lie, that they may destroy him. (D&C 10:25)

If your children believe any of these lies, they may become susceptible to temptation. In contrast, if you teach your children the mind and will of the Lord, they will be able to discern when an idea is of the devil.

Call Your Children to Repentance

You need to be forthright in calling your children to repentance. As you do so in the spirit of love, your children will have a much better chance of abandoning their sins before they become entrenched in a pattern of sin. Here are the words of Moses to fathers:

> Wherefore teach it unto your children, that all men, everywhere, must repent, or they can in nowise inherit the kingdom of God, for no unclean thing can dwell there, or dwell in his presence; for, in the language of Adam, Man of Holiness is his name, and the name of his Only Begotten is the Son of Man, even Jesus Christ, a righteous Judge, who shall come in the meridian of time. (Moses 6:57)

This pattern was followed by Book of Mormon fathers. When it proved necessary, Lehi called his children to repentance:

> And thus Laman and Lemuel, being the eldest, did murmur against their father. And they did murmur because they knew not the dealings of that God who had created them.

75

Neither did they believe that Jerusalem, that great city, could be destroyed according to the words of the prophets. And they were like unto the Jews who were at Jerusalem, who sought to take away the life of my father.

And it came to pass that my father did speak unto them in the valley of Lemuel, with power, being filled with the Spirit, until their frames did shake before him. And he did confound them, that they durst not utter against him; wherefore, they did as he commanded them. (1 Nephi 2:12-14)

• • •

Yea, as one generation passeth to another there shall be bloodsheds, and great visitations among them; wherefore, my sons, I would that ye would remember; yea, I would that ye would hearken unto my words.

O that ye would awake; awake from a deep sleep, yea, even from the sleep of hell, and shake off the chains by which ye are bound, which are the chains which bind the children of men, that they are carried away captive down to the eternal gulf of misery and woe. (2 Nephi 1:12-13)

In the following verses Alma calls his son Corianton to repentance for committing fornication:

And now, my son, I have somewhat more to say unto thee than what I said unto thy brother; for behold, have ye not observed the steadiness of thy brother, his faithfulness, and his diligence in keeping the commandments of God? Behold, has he not set a good example for thee?

For thou didst not give so much heed unto my words as did thy brother, among the people of the Zoramites. Now this is what I have against thee; thou didst go on unto boasting in thy strength and thy wisdom.

And this is not all, my son. Thou didst do that which was grievous unto me; for thou didst forsake the ministry, and did go over into the land of Siron, among the borders of the Lamanites, after the harlot Isabel.

Yea, she did steal away the hearts of many; but this was no excuse for thee, my son. Thou shouldst have tended to the ministry wherewith thou wast entrusted.

Know ye not, my son, that these things are an abomination in the sight of the Lord; yea, most abominable above all sins save it be the shedding of innocent blood or denying the Holy Ghost?

For behold, if ye deny the Holy Ghost when it once has had place in you, and ye know that ye deny it, behold, this is a sin which is unpardonable; yea, and whosoever murdereth against the light and knowledge of God, it is not easy for him to obtain forgiveness; yea, I say unto you, my son, that it is not easy for him to obtain a forgiveness.

And now, my son, I would to God that ye had not been guilty of so great a crime. I would not dwell upon your crimes, to harrow up your soul, if it were not for your good.

But behold, ye cannot hide your crimes from God; and except ye repent they will stand as a testimony against you at the last day.

Now my son, I would that ye should repent and forsake your sins, and go no more after the lusts of your eyes, but cross yourself in all these things; for except ye do this ye can in nowise inherit the kingdom of God. O remember, and take it upon you, and cross yourself in these things. (Alma 39:1-9)

Adam called his children to repentance:

And Adam hearkened unto the voice of God, and called upon his sons to repent. . . . (Moses 6:1)

Review with your children quite frequently two fundamental truths regarding repentance. First, they need to understand that as a result of Jesus Christ's atoning sacrifice they can be forgiven for their sins, and the Lord will remember the sins no more (see D&C 58:42). Second, they need to be taught that their former sins will return if they sin again (see D&C 82:7). For example, if they have stolen something in the past and then steal again, they will be required to confess to their bishop not only their most recent sin, but their past sins as well.

Some young people who become inactive would have remained active if their parents had discerned the first time they sinned and then taken steps to help their children see the error of their ways. All too frequently, young people become entrenched in sins before their parents confront the problem.

Trust the Lord to Guide You

As the patriarch of your home, the Lord will work through you, more than anyone else, to motivate your children to live righteously or repent if necessary. The only thing that would deny you this role is indifference on your part. You should regularly seek inspiration on what you can say and do to motivate your children to keep the commandments. If you do, you will find the Lord quick to inspire you. President Ezra Taft Benson gave fathers the following counsel:

> The father must hunger and thirst and yearn to bless his family; he must go to the Lord, ponder the words of God, and live by the Spirit to know the mind and will of the Lord and what he must do to lead his family. It is soul-satisfying to know that God is mindful of us and ready to respond when we place our trust in Him and do that which is right. (*Teachings of Ezra Taft Benson*, p. 68)

You can be assured that the Lord wants your children to keep the commandments. Trust the Lord to guide you as a patriarch in your efforts to instill in your children a desire to rise above their weaknesses and live righteously.

7

Teach Your Children

Of all the teachers your children will have, you are the most important; you have a very special stewardship. Here are the words of the Lord:

> Therefore I give unto you a commandment, to teach these things freely unto your children, saying:
>
> That by reason of transgression cometh the fall, which fall bringeth death, and inasmuch as ye were born into the world by water, and blood, and the spirit, which I have made, and so become of dust a living soul, even so ye must be born again into the kingdom of heaven, of water, and of the Spirit, and be cleansed by blood, even the blood of mine Only Begotten, that ye might be sanctified from all sin, and enjoy the words of eternal life in the world to come, even immortal glory. (Moses 6:58-59)

• • •

> And again, inasmuch as parents have children in Zion, or in any of her stakes which are organized, that teach them not to understand the doctrine of repentance, faith in Christ the Son of the living God, and

79

of baptism and the gift of the Holy Ghost by the laying on of the hands, when eight years old, the sin be
upon the heads of the parents. (D&C 68:25)

• • •

And they shall also teach their children to pray, and
to walk uprightly before the Lord.

Now, I, the Lord, am not well pleased with the inhabitants of Zion, for there are idlers among them; and
their children are also growing up in wickedness; they
also seek not earnestly the riches of eternity, but their
eyes are full of greediness. (D&C 68:28, 31)

In speaking to his three sons, King Benjamin said he and
other fathers had taught their children the gospel to fulfill the
commandments of God (see Mosiah 1:4). In speaking to
fathers generally about their responsibility to teach their children, King Benjamin said:

Neither will ye suffer that they transgress the laws of
God, and fight and quarrel one with another, and
serve the devil, who is the master of sin, or who is the
evil spirit which hath been spoken of by our fathers,
he being an enemy to all righteousness.

But ye will teach them to walk in the ways of truth
and soberness; ye will teach them to love one another, and to serve one another. (Mosiah 4:14-15)

Here are the words of a modern-day prophet:

The greatest blessing we can give our children and
that can be extended to all the children of the world
will come though the simple processes of teaching
and training them in the way of the Lord.

Home life, proper teaching in the home, parental
guidance and leadership—these are the panacea for
the ailments of the world and its children. They are
the cure for spiritual and emotional diseases and the
remedy for its problems. Parents should not leave the
training of children to others.

The Doctrine and Covenants makes it very clear. It is the responsibility of the parents to teach their children. All other agencies are secondary. If parents do not teach their children—their children—they will be held responsible. (Spencer W. Kimball, *Ensign*, May 1979, p. 5)

Fathers Have the Major Responsibility for Teaching Their Children

Because you are the patriarch, you have the major responsibility to teach your children how to conduct their lives and how to look to Christ for a remission of their sins (see 2 Nephi 25:6). President Ezra Taft Benson summarizes this responsibility:

> One of the great needs is more parental instruction in life's problems. I know there is a tendency for parents to shrink from this responsibility, the instructing of their own children in the problems of sex, the relationship with other young people, the problem of dating, and all of the many temptations that confront a growing boy and girl. These instructions should not be left to the school or to a class in sociology. The safest place, the best place, to give this vital counsel, these sacred instructions in matters of moral purity, should be in the home on a basis of confidence between parent and child. As parents, we should instruct our children. The sacred books of the ancient Persians say: "If you would be holy, instruct your children, because all the good acts they perform will be imputed unto you." (*So Shall You Reap*, pp. 120-121)

• • •

What should we teach? The Lord has revealed the specific curriculum that parents should teach. Note His words: "Teach it unto your children, that all men, everywhere, must repent, or they can in nowise inherit the kingdom of God, for no unclean thing can dwell there, or dwell in his presence."

81

As further noted in this scripture, the fundamental doctrines consist of the doctrine of the Fall, the mission of Christ and His atonement, and the first principles and ordinances of the gospel, which include faith in Christ, repentance, baptism for a remission of sins, and the gift of the Holy Ghost as the means to a sanctified life. (*Come Unto Christ*, p. 60)

You will err in your role as a patriarch if you leave your wife or others the sole responsibility of shaping your children's ideas and standards.

From the writings of the sons of Helaman, we see that a father's teachings can have a profound influence on his children:

And it came to pass that Nephi had become weary because of their iniquity; and he yielded up the judgment-seat, and took it upon him to preach the word of God all the remainder of his days, and his brother Lehi also, all the remainder of his days;

For they remembered the words which their father Helaman spake unto them. And these are the words which he spake:

Behold, my sons, I desire that ye should remember to keep the commandments of God; and I would that ye should declare unto the people these words. Behold, I have given unto you the names of our first parents who came out of the land of Jerusalem; and this I have done that when you remember your names ye may remember them; and when ye remember them, ye may remember their works; and when ye remember their works ye may know how that it is said, and also written, that they were good.

Therefore, my sons, I would that ye should do that which is good, that it may be said of you, and also written, even as it has been said and written of them.

And now my sons, behold I have somewhat more to desire of you, which desire is, that ye may not do these things that ye may boast, but that ye may do these things to lay up for yourselves a treasure in heaven, yea, which is eternal, and which fadeth not away; yea, that ye may have that precious gift of eternal life, which we have reason to suppose hath been given to our fathers.

O remember, remember, my sons, the words which King Benjamin spake unto his people; yea, remember that there is no other way nor means whereby man can be saved, only through the atoning blood of Jesus Christ, who shall come; yea, remember that he cometh to redeem the world.

And remember also the words which Amulek spake unto Zeezrom, in the city of Ammonihah; for he said unto him that the Lord surely should come to redeem his people, but that he should not come to redeem them in their sins, but to redeem them from their sins.

And he hath power given unto him from the Father to redeem them from their sins because of repentance; therefore he hath sent his angels to declare the tidings of the conditions of repentance, which bringeth unto the power of the Redeemer, unto the salvation of their souls.

And now, my sons, remember, remember that it is upon the rock of our Redeemer, who is Christ, the son of God, that ye must build your foundation; that when the devil shall send forth his mighty winds, yea, his shafts in the whirlwind, yea, when all his hail and his mighty storm shall beat upon you, it shall have no power over you to drag you down to the gulf of misery and endless wo, because of the rock upon which ye are built, which is a sure foundation, a foundation whereon if men build they cannot fall.

And it came to pass that these were the words which Helaman taught to his sons; yea, he did teach them many things which are not written, and also many things which are written.

And they did remember his words; and therefore they went forth, keeping the commandments of God, to teach the word of God among all the people of Nephi, beginning at the city Bountiful. (Helaman 5:4-14)

These verses illustrate several important lessons: (a) the powerful influence of a family name (verse 6), (b) the influence of children being taught about their ancestors (verse 7), (c) the influence of a father's righteous desires on his children (verse 8), (d) the effect of a father quoting his forefathers to his children (verses 9-11), (e) the influence of a father's testimony on his children (verse 12), (f) the influence of a father's teachings on his children (verse 13), and (g) the teachings of a father helping his children become more effective missionaries (verses 14-19).

Teach Fundamental Truths

Three fundamental truths, if grasped and understood, will ensure that your children remain faithful to the teachings and precepts of the gospel:

- *A personal witness that God does exist.*
- *A comprehensive understanding of God's character.*
- *An assurance that their thoughts, words, and actions are in accord with the mind and will of God.*

The prophet Joseph Smith warned:

Without an acquaintance with these three important facts, the faith of every rational being must be imperfect; but with this understanding it can become perfect and faithful, abounding in righteousness. (*Lectures on Faith*, p. 33)

On another occasion he said:

Without these ideas being planted in the minds of men, it would be out of power of any person or persons to exercise faith in God. (*Lectures on Faith*, p. 43)

Your children need to be taught the following specifics regarding God:

- *God is merciful, gracious, slow to anger, abundant in goodness, and has always possessed these attributes.*

- *God does not change. He is the same "from everlasting to everlasting," being the same yesterday, today, and forever.*

- *God is a God of truth and cannot lie.*

- *God is no respecter of persons, and if anyone will live righteously they will be accepted by Him.*

- *God is a God of love.*

- *God is pleased when we live righteously.*

- *God's sole purpose is to help us attain eternal life.*

These scriptures can guide you in fulfilling your responsibilities to teach your children about God:

Exodus 34:6	Psalms 103:6-8	Psalms 103:17, 18
Psalms 90:2	Hebrews 1:10-12	James 1:17
Malachi 3:6	D&C 3:2	D&C 35:1
Acts 10:34-35	Moses 1:39	Mosiah 4:9
2 Nephi 27:23	Moroni 7:12	2 Nephi 2:6
2 Nephi 9:20	1 Nephi 8:8	2 Nephi 27:23
Mosiah 4:9	1 Nephi 9:6	2 Nephi 29:7
Ether 3:12	Alma 9:26	Moroni 8:18

Consistently Teach Your Children the Gospel of Jesus Christ

A true patriarch systematically teaches his children the gospel of Jesus Christ. As you read the Book of Mormon, you will discover that righteous fathers like Lehi and Alma had a comprehensive knowledge of the gospel and the scriptures. By reading the scriptures daily and studying the general conference reports in depth, your knowledge of the gospel of Jesus Christ will enable you to teach your children the gospel.

Lehi taught his children the gospel of Jesus Christ:

> For behold, it came to pass after my father had made an end of speaking the words of his dream, and also of exhorting them to all diligence, he spake unto them concerning the Jews—
>
> That after they should be destroyed, even that great city Jerusalem, and many be carried away captive into Babylon, according to the own due time of the Lord, they should return again, yea, even be brought back out of captivity; and after they should be brought back out of captivity they should possess again the land of their inheritance.
>
> Yea, even six hundred years from the time that my father left Jerusalem, a prophet would the Lord God raise up among the Jews—even a Messiah, or, in other words, a Savior of the world.
>
> And he also spake concerning the prophets, how great a number had testified of these things, concerning this Messiah, of whom he had spoken, or this Redeemer of the world.
>
> Wherefore, all mankind were in a lost and in a fallen state, and ever would be save they should rely on this Redeemer.
>
> And he spake also concerning a prophet who should come before the Messiah, to prepare the way of the Lord—
>
> Yea, even he should go forth and cry in the wilderness: Prepare ye the way of the Lord, and make his paths straight; for there standeth one among you whom ye know not; and he is mightier than I, whose shoe's latchet I am not worthy to unloose. And much spake my father concerning this thing.
>
> And my father said he should baptize in Bethabara, beyond Jordan; and he also said he should baptize with water; even that he should baptize the Messiah with water.

And after he had baptized the Messiah with water, he should behold and bear record that he had baptized the Lamb of God, who should take away the sins of the world.

And it came to pass after my father had spoken these words he spake unto my brethren concerning the gospel which should be preached among the Jews, and also concerning the dwindling of the Jews in unbelief. And after they had slain the Messiah, who should come, and after he had been slain he should rise from the dead, and should make himself manifest, by the Holy Ghost, unto the Gentiles. (1 Nephi 10:2-11)

Alma taught one of his sons about the state of the spirit following death:

Now, concerning the state of the soul between death and the resurrection—Behold, it has been made known unto me by an angel, that the spirits of all men, as soon as they are departed from this mortal body, yea, the spirits of all men, whether they be good or evil, are taken home to that God who gave them life.

And then shall it come to pass, that the spirits of those who are righteous are received into a state of happiness, which is called paradise, a state of rest, a state of peace, where they shall rest from all their troubles and from all care, and sorrow.

And then shall it come to pass, that the spirits of the wicked, yea, who are evil—for behold, they have no part nor portion of the Spirit of the Lord; for behold, they chose evil works rather than good; therefore the spirit of the devil did enter into them, and take possession of their house—and these shall be cast out into outer darkness; there shall be weeping, and wailing, and gnashing of teeth, and this because of their own iniquity, being led captive by the will of the devil.

> Now this is the state of the souls of the wicked, yea,
> in darkness, and a state of awful, fearful looking for
> the fiery indignation of the wrath of God upon them;
> thus they remain in this state, as well as the righteous
> in paradise, until the time of their resurrection.
> (Alma 40:11-14)

As a patriarch to your children, you would be well advised
to follow Alma's example and start teaching your children the
gospel of Jesus Christ when they are very young (see Alma
36:3). Young children are very receptive to truth. Lehi said
his son Jacob beheld the Lord's glory in his youth (see 2
Nephi 2:4).

In teaching your children the gospel, you should focus on
some doctrines more than others; all truths are not of equal
value. The most important truths are the saving truths of salvation. Follow the pattern of Book of Mormon patriarchs and
focus on the fall, atonement, rebirth, resurrection, judgment,
and eternal life.

It is paramount that your children understand the mission
of Jesus Christ; that he was literally the Son of God, that he
came to earth, established the Church and kingdom, and
finally gave his life for the sins of mankind, thus making it
possible for us to enjoy immortality and eternal life. They
need to be taught that God is a loving Father who hears and
answers prayers. Strive to teach these basic truths plainly, frequently, and fervently. It would be wise to follow the counsel
of President Ezra Taft Benson:

> Repetition is the key to learning. Our children need
> to hear the truth repeated, especially because there is
> so much falsehood abroad. (*Ensign*, Nov. 1985, p. 36)

We learn a very important lesson from Helaman's example
in teaching his children the gospel. There are two great sermons in the Book of Mormon that should receive special
emphasis. Here are Helaman's words:

> O remember, remember, my sons, the words which
> king Benjamin spake unto his people; yea, remember

that there is no other way nor means whereby man can be saved, only through the atoning blood of Jesus Christ, who shall come, yea, remember that he cometh to redeem the world.

And remember also the words which Amulek spake unto Zeezrom, in the city of Ammonihah; for he said unto him that the Lord surely should come to redeem his people, but that he should not come to redeem them in their sins, but to redeem them from their sins. (Helaman 5:9-10)

King Benjamin's sermon is recorded in Mosiah, consisting of chapters 2 through 4. Amulek's testimony to Zeezrom is found in the 11th chapter of the Book of Alma.

Teach Your Children About Their Ancestors

In addition to teaching your children the saving doctrines of the gospel of Jesus Christ, and to forsake all forms of unrighteousness, you should also teach your children about their ancestors.

In the Book of Mormon we see examples of fathers teachings their children about their forefathers. Also, we see the importance of children studying the genealogy of their forefathers. This is one of the reasons why the Lord commanded Lehi to send his sons back to Jerusalem to get the plates from Laban (see 1 Nephi 5:14-19). The following verses explain the significance of Lehi and his family having the genealogy of their forefathers:

And it came to pass that my father, Lehi, also found upon the plates of brass a genealogy of his fathers; wherefore he knew that he was a descendant of Joseph; yea, even that Joseph who was the son of Jacob, who was sold into Egypt, and who was preserved by the hand of the Lord, that he might preserve his father, Jacob, and all his household from perishing with famine.

And they were also led out of captivity and out of the land of Egypt, by the same God who had preserved them.

89

> And thus my father, Lehi, did discover the genealogy of his father. And Laban also was a descendant of Joseph, wherefore he and his fathers had kept the records.
>
> And now when my father saw all these things, he was filled with the Spirit, and began to prophesy concerning his seed.
>
> That these plates of brass should go forth unto all nations, kindreds, tongues, and people who were of his seed.
>
> Wherefore, he said that these plates of brass should never perish; neither should they be dimmed any more by time. And he prophesied many things concerning his seed. (1 Nephi 5:14-19)

Throughout history, righteous fathers maintained a genealogy of their forefathers (see Moses 6:45-46; Alma 37:3; Jarom 1:1; Omni 1:1; Omni 1:18; Ether 1:6-32). This pattern was revealed to Adam:

> Now this prophecy Adam spake, as he was moved upon by the Holy Ghost, and a genealogy was kept of the children of God. And this was the book of the generations of Adam, saying: In the day that God created man, in the likeness of God made he him. (Moses 6:8)

It is very important that children have a sense of identity with their forefathers and a feeling of pride regarding their heritage. In spite of whatever weaknesses their grandparents and great-grandparents may have had, children should be taught about the positive traits of their ancestors.

If children are taught about their ancestors, their "hearts" will turn to their forefathers, and they will realize that their ancestors in the spirit world can sustain and help them in their mortal endeavors. Elder Vaughn J. Featherstone has explained that temple attendance invites the influence of departed spirits to bless your children:

> I promise you that all who faithfully attend to the temple work will be blessed beyond measure. Your

families will draw closer to the Lord. Unseen angels will watch over your loved ones when satanic forces tempt them. The veil will be thin, and great spiritual experiences will distill upon this people. (As quoted by Sister Maxine Cameron, matron of the Provo Temple.)

Knowing that those beyond the veil may exercise faith in their behalf can be a real source of strength to your children throughout their lives.

Clarify Misconceptions Regarding Gospel Doctrines

From the writings of righteous Book of Mormon fathers, we see that a father has the responsibility to clarify his children's misconceptions regarding the doctrines associated with the gospel of Jesus Christ. For example, Alma's son Corianton had some serious misconceptions about the resurrection, and Alma went to great lengths to correct his misconceptions. The following verses are excerpts from what Alma said to his son about this doctrine:

And now, my son, I have somewhat to say concerning the restoration of which has been spoken; for behold, some have wrested the scriptures, and have gone far astray because of this thing. And I perceive that thy mind has been worried also concerning this thing. But behold, I will explain it unto thee.

I say unto thee, my son, that the plan of restoration is requisite with the justice of God; for it is requisite that all things should be restored to their proper order. Behold, it is requisite and just, according to the power and resurrection of Christ, that the soul of man should be restored to its body, and that every part of the body should be restored to itself.

And it is requisite with the justice of God that men should be judged according to their works; and if their works were good in this life, and the desires of their hearts were good, that they should also, at the last day, be restored unto that which is good.

And if their works are evil they shall be restored unto
them for evil. Therefore, all things shall be restored
to their proper order, every thing to its natural
frame—mortality raised to immortality, corruption to
incorruption—raised to endless happiness to inherit
the kingdom of God, or to endless misery to inherit
the kingdom of the devil, the one on one hand, the
other on the other—

The one raised to happiness according to his desires
of happiness, or good according to his desires of good;
and the other to evil according to his desires of evil;
for as he has desired to do evil all the day long even
so shall he have his reward of evil when the night
cometh. (Alma 41:1-5)

A classic example of a father clarifying misconceptions
regarding church doctrine is found in one of Mormon's letters
to his son Moroni:

For, if I have learned the truth, there have been disputations among you concerning the baptism of your
little children. And now, my son, I desire that ye
should labor diligently, that this gross error should be
removed from among you; for, for this intent I have
written this epistle.

For immediately after I had learned these things of
you I inquired of the Lord concerning the matter.
And the word of the Lord came to me by the power
of the Holy Ghost, saying:

Listen to the words of Christ, your Redeemer, your
Lord and your God. Behold, I came into the world
not to call the righteous but sinners to repentance;
the whole need no physician, but they that are sick;
wherefore, little children are whole, for they are not
capable of committing sin; wherefore the curse of
Adam is taken from them in me, that it hath no
power over them; and the law of circumcision is done
away in me.

And after this manner did the Holy Ghost manifest
the word of God unto me; wherefore, my beloved

son, I know that it is solemn mockery before God, that ye should baptize little children.

Behold I say unto you that this thing shall ye teach—repentance and baptism unto those who are accountable and capable of committing sin; yea, teach parents that they must repent and be baptized, and humble themselves as their little children, and they shall all be saved with their little children.

And their little children need no repentance, neither baptism. Behold, baptism is unto repentance to the fulfilling the commandments unto the remission of sins.

But little children are alive in Christ, even from the foundation of the world; if not so, God is a partial God, and also a changeable God, and a respecter to persons; for how many little children have died without baptism!

Wherefore, if little children could not be saved without baptism, these must have gone to an endless hell.

Behold I say unto you, that he that supposeth that little children need baptism is in the gall of bitterness and in the bonds of iniquity, for he hath neither faith, hope, nor charity; wherefore, should he be cut off while in the thought, he must go down to hell.

For awful is the wickedness to suppose that God saveth one child because of baptism, and the other must perish because he hath no baptism.

Wo be unto them that shall pervert the ways of the Lord after this manner, for they shall perish except they repent. Behold, I speak with boldness, having authority from God; and I fear not what man can do; for perfect love casteth out all fear.

And I am filled with charity, which is everlasting love; wherefore, all children are alike unto me; wherefore, I love little children with a perfect love; and they are all alike and partakers of salvation.

For I know that God is not a partial God, neither a changeable being; but he is unchangeable from all eternity to all eternity.

Little children cannot repent; wherefore, it is awful wickedness to deny the pure mercies of God unto them, for they are all alive in him because of his mercy.

And he that saith that little children need baptism denieth the mercies of Christ, and setteth at naught the atonement of him and the power of his redemption.

Wo unto such, for they are in danger of death, hell, and an endless torment. I speak it boldly; God hath commanded me. Listen unto them and give heed, or they stand against you at the judgment-seat of Christ.

For behold that all little children are alive in Christ, and also all they that are without the law. For the power of redemption cometh on all them that have no law; wherefore, he that is not condemned, or he that is under no condemnation, cannot repent; and unto such baptism availeth nothing—

But it is mockery before God, denying the mercies of Christ, and the power of his Holy Spirit, and putting trust in dead works. (Moroni 8:5-23)

Quite often children misunderstand things they hear in lessons or talks and consequently form misconceptions. As a patriarch, you have two responsibilities: first, you need to be alert and perceptive in identifying misconceptions your children have regarding church doctrine or policy; second, you need to take the necessary steps to correct these misconceptions. Otherwise, misconceptions may result in serious consequences in the lives of your children.

Teach Your Children to Love and Serve Each Other

The teachings of King Benjamin can help fathers understand some of the topics they should focus on in their effort to teach their children:

> And ye will not suffer your children that they go hungry, or naked; neither will ye suffer that they transgress the laws of God, and fight and quarrel one with another, and serve the devil, who is the master of sin, or who is the evil spirit which hath been spoken of by our fathers, he being an enemy to all righteousness.

> But ye will teach them to walk in the ways of truth and soberness; ye will teach them to love one another, and to serve one another. (Mosiah 4:14-15)

If you successfully get your children to refrain from quarreling and to love and serve each other, you will have accomplished one of your major responsibilities as a patriarch. If your family collectively works to succor those in need and to share your substance with the needy, the spirit of the priesthood will abound in your home (see Mosiah 4:16, 26; Mosiah 2:17).

Teach Your Children the Importance of the Scriptures

Unless you specifically teach your children the importance of the scriptures, there is a danger that your children will not develop an affinity for them. All too frequently fathers fail to realize this is their responsibility, not making a systematic effort to instill in their children a love for the scriptures. Children need to understand that if it were not for the scriptures, they would "suffer in ignorance" (Mosiah 1:3).

Alma, as a patriarch, taught his children to realize the importance of the scriptures. The following verses are examples from his writings:

> Behold, it has been prophesied by our fathers, that they should be kept and handed down from one generation to another, and be kept and preserved by the hand of the Lord until they should go forth unto every nation, kindred, tongue, and people, that they shall know of the mysteries contained thereon.

> And now behold, if they are kept they must retain their brightness; yea, and they will retain their

brightness; yea, and also shall all the plates which do contain that which is holy writ.

Now ye may suppose that this is foolishness in me; but behold I say unto you, that by small and simple things are great things brought to pass; and small means in many instances doth confound the wise.

And the Lord God doth work by means to bring about his great and eternal purposes; and by very small means the Lord doth confound the wise and bringeth about the salvation of many souls.

And now, it has hitherto been wisdom in God that these things should be preserved; for behold, they have enlarged the memory of this people, yea, and convinced many of the error of their ways, and brought them to the knowledge of their God unto the salvation of their souls.

Yea, I say unto you, were it not for these things that these records do contain, which are on these plates, Ammon and his brethren could not have convinced so many thousands of the Lamanites of the incorrect tradition of their fathers; yea, these records and their words brought them unto repentance; that is, they brought them to the knowledge of the Lord their God, and to rejoice in Jesus Christ their Redeemer.

And who knoweth but what they will be the means of bringing many thousands of them, yea, and also many thousands of our stiff-necked brethren, the Nephites, who are now hardening their hearts in sin and iniquities, to the knowledge of their Redeemer? (Alma 37:4-10)

• • •

And now remember, my son, that God has entrusted you with these things, which are sacred, which he has kept sacred, and also which he will keep and preserve for a wise purpose in him, that he may show forth his power unto future generations.

And now behold, I tell you by the spirit of prophecy, that if ye transgress the commandments of God, behold, these things which are sacred shall be taken away from you by the power of God, and ye shall be delivered up unto Satan, that he may sift you as chaff before the wind.

But if ye keep the commandments of God, and do with these things which are sacred according to that which the Lord doth command you, (for you must appeal unto the Lord for all things whatsoever ye must do with them) behold, no power of earth or hell can take them from you, for God is powerful to the fulfilling of all his words.

For he will fulfil all his promises which he shall make unto you, for he has fulfilled his promises which he has made unto our fathers.

For he promised unto them that he would reserve these things for a wise purpose in him, that he might show forth his power unto future generations.

And now behold, one purpose hath he fulfilled, even to the restoration of many thousands of Lamanites to the knowledge of the truth; and he hath shown forth his power in them, and he will also still show forth his power in them unto future generations; therefore they shall be preserved. (Alma 37:14-19)

Lehi taught his children the importance of the scriptures. The following verses relate what he did once his sons had successfully obtained the brass plates from Laban:

And after they had given thanks unto the God of Israel, my father, Lehi, took the records which were engraven upon the plates of brass, and he did search them from the beginning.

And he beheld that they did contain the five books of Moses, which gave an account of the creation of the world,and also of Adam and Eve, who were our first parents;

And also a record of the Jews from the beginning, even down to the commencement of the reign of Zedekiah, king of Judah;

And also the prophecies of the holy prophets, from the beginning, even down to the commencement of the reign of Zedekiah; and also many prophecies which have been spoken by the mouth of Jeremiah.

And it came to pass that my father, Lehi, also found upon the plates of brass a genealogy of his fathers; wherefore he knew that he was a descendant of Joseph; yea, even that Joseph who was the son of Jacob, who was sold into Egypt, and who was preserved by the hand of the Lord, that he might preserve his father, Jacob, and all his household from perishing with famine.

And they were also led out of captivity and out of the land of Egypt, by that same God who had preserved them.

And thus my father, Lehi, did discover the genealogy of his fathers. And Laban also was a descendant of Joseph, wherefore he and his fathers had kept the records.

And now when my father saw all these things, he was filled with the Spirit, and began to prophesy concerning his seed—

That these plates of brass should go forth unto all nations, kindreds, tongues, and people who were of his seed.

Wherefore, he said that these plates of brass should never perish; neither should they be dimmed any more by time. And he prophesied many things concerning his seed.

And it came to pass that thus far I and my father had kept the commandments wherewith the Lord had commanded us.

And we had obtained the records which the Lord had commanded us, and searched them and found that they were desirable; yea, even of great worth unto us, insomuch that we could preserve the commandments of the Lord unto our children.

Wherefore, it was wisdom in the Lord that we should carry them with us, as we journeyed in the wilderness towards the land of promise. (1 Nephi 5:10-22)

King Benjamin explained to his children that if it were not for the scriptures, they would dwindle in unbelief:

My sons, I would that you should remember that if it were not for these plates which contain these records and these commandments, we must have suffered in ignorance even at this present time, not knowing the mysteries of God.

For it were not possible that our father, Lehi, could have remembered all these things, to have taught them to his children, except it were for the help of these plates; for he having been taught in the language of the Egyptians therefore he could read these engravings, and teach them to his children, they could teach them to their children, and so fulfilling the commandments of God, even down to this present time.

I say unto you, my sons, were it not for these things, which have been kept and preserved by the hand of God, that we might read and understand of his mysteries and have his commandments always before our eyes, that even our fathers would have dwindled in unbelief, and we should have been like unto our brethren, the Lamanites, who know nothing concerning these things, or even do not believe them when they are taught them, because of the traditions of their fathers, which are not correct. (Mosiah 1:3-5)

It is very important that your children become aware of the hand of the Lord in the scriptures being compiled and preserved, especially his effort to ensure that we have various volumes of scriptures at our disposal during this last dispensation. No other people in the history of the world have enjoyed the advantages of multiple volumes of scriptures as we do today.

Teach Your Children to Search the Scriptures Diligently

Of all the things your children can do to enhance their spirituality, scripture study is probably the most important. In those instances when fathers succeed in teaching their children to delight in the scriptures, the children are much more successful in coping with the challenges of youth. Your goal should be to teach your children to "feast upon the words of Christ" (see 2 Nephi 32:3). As a prophet, Spencer W. Kimball stressed this point:

> I am convinced that each of us . . . must discover the scriptures for ourselves . . . and not just discover them once, but rediscover them again and again. (*Ensign*, Sept. 1976, p. 4)

King Benjamin admonished his children to search the scriptures diligently, promising them that they would "profit" from their knowledge of the scriptures (see Mosiah 1:7). Children need to be taught that no matter how faithful they are in other respects, certain blessings will be lost if they do not study the scriptures. Here are the words of a modern-day prophet:

> Success in righteousness, the power to avoid deception and resist temptation, guidance in our daily lives, healing of the soul—these are but a few of the promises the Lord has given to those who come to His word. Does the Lord promise and not fulfill? Surely if He tells us these things will come to us if we lay hold upon His word, then the blessings can be ours. And if we do not, the blessings may be lost. However diligent we may be in other areas, certain blessings are to be found only in the scriptures, only in coming to the word of the Lord and holding fast to it as we make our way through the mists of darkness to the tree of life.

And if we ignore what the Lord has given us, we may lose the very power and blessings which we seek. In a solemn warning to the early Saints the Lord said this of the Book of Mormon: "Your minds at times have been darkened because of unbelief, and because you have treated lightly the things you have received—

"Which vanity and unbelief have brought the whole church under condemnation.

"And this condemnation resteth upon the children of Zion, even all.

"And they shall remain under this condemnation until they repent and remember the new covenant, even the Book of Mormon." (D&C 84:55-57)

O my brethren, let us not treat lightly the great things we have received from the hand of the Lord! His word is one of the most valuable gifts He has given us. I urge you to recommit yourselves to a study of the scriptures. (President Ezra Taft Benson, *Ensign*, May 1986, p. 82)

Your children need to understand that even though they study all of the scriptures, they should make it a practice to read from the Book of Mormon daily. President Ezra Taft Benson has counseled:

Of the four great standard works of the church . . . the Bible, the Book of Mormon, the Doctrine and Covenants and the Pearl of Great Price—I would particularly urge you to read again and again the Book of Mormon and to ponder and apply its teachings. (*Ensign*, May 1986, p. 43)

• • •

We must make the Book of Mormon a center focus of study because it was written for our day. The Nephites never had the book; neither did the Lamanites of ancient times. It was meant for us. Mormon wrote near the end of the Nephite civilization. Under the inspiration of God, who sees all things from the beginning, he abridged centuries of records, choosing the stories, speeches, and events that would be most helpful to us. (*Teachings of Ezra Taft Benson*, p. 58)

Speaking to parents President Ezra Taft Benson warned:

Now, we have not been using the Book of Mormon as we should. Our homes are not as strong unless we are using it to bring our children to Christ. Our families may be corrupted by worldly trends and teachings unless we know how to use the book to expose and combat the falsehoods in socialism, organic evolution, rationalism, humanism, and so forth. (*A Witness and a Warning*, p. 6)

On another occasion President Ezra Taft Benson counseled fathers to instruct their children about the Book of Mormon "[at their] dinner table, [by their] firesides, at their bedsides, and in [their] letters and phone calls—in all of [their] goings and comings (*A Witness and a Warning*, p. 11). Strive to help your children see the importance of filling their minds with righteous principles.

If we would escape the lusts of the flesh, and build for ourselves, and for our children great and noble characters, we must keep in our minds and in their minds true and righteous principles for our thoughts and their thoughts to dwell upon.

We must not permit our minds to become surfeited with the interests, things, and practices of the world about us.

If we would avoid adopting the evils of the world, we must pursue a course which will daily feed our minds with and call them back to the things of the spirit. I know of no better way to do this than by reading the Book of Mormon. (Marion G. Romney, *Conference Report*, April 1960, p. 111)

Anciently Nephi prophesied that our generations would have the Book of Mormon and "shall be judged . . . according to the words that are written" (2 Nephi 25:22). Knowing that you and your family are going to be judged by what is written in the Book of Mormon gives you a compelling reason to read it.

Moroni promised that you would learn the "decrees of God" from the Book of Mormon, and by obedience to them escape the calamities of the last days (Ether 2:11). You have the assurance that as your children live by the precepts of the Book of Mormon, they will learn to discern truth and will not be deceived by false doctrines or false teachings of men. More than anything else, the Book of Mormon will fortify your children against evil.

Over the years, President Ezra Taft Benson has cited specific blessings your children will obtain as they read from the Book of Mormon each day:

- *They will be blessed with the power to avoid deception and resist temptation.*
- *Mutual respect and consideration for other family members will grow.*
- *The ability to understand the teachings of the Book of Mormon will increase.*
- *They will become more responsible and submissive to the counsel of their parents.*
- *They will develop a closer relationship with Christ.*
- *They will be blessed with added power to endure in righteousness amidst the growing onslaught of wickedness.*
- *Their ability to receive personal revelation to bless the lives of others will increase.*
- *They will experience joy and happiness.*
- *It will fortify them against the evils of our day.*
- *It will bring spirituality into their lives.*
- *They will be able to stand against the wiles of the devil.*
- *Reading the Book of Mormon will heal their souls.*

Review these promises with your children frequently. Doing this not only will help ensure that your children will study the Book of Mormon, but it will also increase their faith that the Lord will bless them for their efforts.

As your children establish a pattern of reading the scriptures every day, in time they will learn to delight in the scriptures. But most important, the teachings in the scriptures will guide their conduct. Here is the promise of a prophet:

> The more we are familiar with the scriptures, the closer we become to the mind and will of the Lord. It will be easier for us to allow the truths of eternity to rest on our minds. (*Teachings of Ezra Taft Benson*, p. 40)

Teach Your Children to Bridle Their Tongues

As a patriarch follow King Benjamin's example in teaching your children that improper language is a serious sin and can jeopardize their eternal salvation (see Mosiah 4:30). Children of all ages need to be taught that many forms of speech besides profanity offend the Lord. For example, the Lord abhors a liar (see Psalms 119:163). Teenagers have a tendency to condone suggestive humor, sarcasm, and fault-finding. As a patriarch go to great lengths to help your children realize that if they use any language that is offensive to the Lord, their spirituality will be impeded to some degree.

Encourage your children to use language that conforms to the Lord's strict standard: "Strengthen your brethren in all your conversations" (D&C 108:7); "Cease to find fault one with another" (D&C 84:24); "Let no corrupt communications proceed out of your mouth" (Eph. 4:29); "neither filthiness, nor foolish talking nor jesting" (Eph. 5:4). If your children comply with the Lord's standard, they will not make sarcastic remarks about other people, or use humor that is off-colored or belittling.

Your children's incidental conversations are a measure of their character:

> Who is a wise man and endued with knowledge among you? Let him shew out of a good conversation his works with meekness of wisdom. (James 3:13)

• • •

> If you wish a man to portray himself faithfully, you must get him to talk, and I will ensure you the organs of speech will show out the true state of the mind sooner or later, and reveal the fruit of his heart. No mind can hide if he is allowed to talk. He will be sure to manifest his true feelings. (Brigham Young, *Journal of Discourses*, 3:237)

Children need to be taught that the Lord will hold them accountable for inappropriate conversations:

> But I say unto you, That every idle word that men shall speak, they shall give account thereof in the day of judgment.
>
> For by thy words thou shalt be justified, and by thy words thou shalt be condemned. (Matt. 12:36-37)

• • •

> Not that which goeth into the mouth defileth a man; but that which cometh out of the mouth, this defileth a man. (Matt. 15:11)

• • •

> For our words will condemn us, yea, all our works will condemn us; we shall not be found spotless; and our thoughts will also condemn us; and in this awful state we shall not dare to look up to our God; and we would fain be glad if we could command the rocks and the mountains to fall upon us to hide us from his presence. (Alma 12:14)

When children learn to bridle their tongues, they will be blessed with good judgment (decisions influenced by inspiration). President Brigham Young said the following about the relationship between appropriate language and good judgment:

> If you gain power to check your words, you will then begin to have the power to check your judgment. (*Journal of Discourses*, 6:98)

If your children successfully refrain from language that offends the Lord, the Lord has promised that in time the spirit will help them overcome their wickedness:

> For in many things we offend all. If any man offend not in word, the same is a perfect man, and able also to bridle the whole body. (James 3:2)

Teach Your Children the Significance of Their Spiritual Heritage

The scriptures frequently refer to the House of Israel. It is important that a father understand the inception of the House of Israel, how a person becomes a member of the House of Israel, the significance of the Abrahamic covenant, who is considered a descendant of Abraham (see D&C 84:33-34; D&C 103:117; D&C 138:41), and the role of the House of Israel in establishing Zion in the world.

But most important, a father needs to help his children realize the blessings they are entitled to as a result of being a member of the House of Israel. Not only should a father become knowledgeable regarding the House of Israel, he should help his children comprehend the significance of being members of the House of Israel. Before baptism, children need to be taught that as a result of being born under the new and everlasting covenant, they are entitled to some of the blessings associated with the House of Israel. Following baptism, they are entitled to additional blessings. Finally, as they receive their temple endowments and are married for time and all eternity, they are entitled to all of the blessings associated with the House of Israel.

Lehi's writings show the importance of a father teaching his children of their spiritual heritage and the significance of being a part of the House of Israel.

Yea, even my father spake much concerning the Gentiles, and also concerning the house of Israel, that they should be compared like unto an olive-tree, whose branches would be broken off and should be scattered upon all the face of the earth.

Wherefore, he said it must needs be that we should be led with one accord into the land of promise, unto the fulfilling of the word of the Lord, that we should be scattered upon all the face of the earth.

And after the house of Israel should be scattered they should be gathered together again; or, in fine, after the Gentiles had received the fulness of the Gospel, the natural branches of the olive-tree, or the remnants of the house of Israel, should be grafted in, or come to the knowledge of the true Messiah, their Lord and their Redeemer. (1 Nephi 10:12-14)

• • •

Wherefore, our father hath not spoken of our seed alone, but also of all the House of Israel, pointing to the covenant which should be fulfilled in the latter days; which covenant the Lord made to our father Abraham, saying; In thy seed shall all the kindreds of the earth be blessed. (1 Nephi 15:18)

• • •

For behold, thou art the fruit of my loins; and I am a descendant of Joseph who was carried captive into Egypt. And great were the covenants of the Lord which he made unto Joseph. (2 Nephi 3:4)

• • •

Wherefore, because of this covenant thou art blessed; for thy seed shall not be destroyed, for they shall hearken unto the words of the book. (2 Nephi 3:23)

You should make it a practice to review and discuss the following references with your children on a fairly regular basis:

1 Nephi 10:14	1 Nephi 19:8-19	1 Nephi 22:1-28
Isaiah 5:26	2 Nephi 29:1-2	2 Nephi 30:8

2 Nephi 33:13	Isaiah 11:12	Jacob 5:1-77
Jacob 6:1-8	Alma 26:37	Isaiah 2:2-3
3 Nephi 16:11-15	3 Nephi 20:16-40	3 Nephi 21:1-28
Daniel 2:34-35	3 Nephi 23:1-4	3 Nephi 29:1-9
Mormon 3:17-22	Daniel 2:44-45	D&C 65:2-6
D&C 10:65	D&C 29:7	D&C:39:11

The Lord has stipulated that the Book of Mormon is to be "A standard unto my people, which are of the house of Israel" (2 Nephi 29:2).

Once your children understand the promises associated with the House of Israel, they will be able to see the "big picture"—the earth being prepared for the Savior's second coming. In the Lord's dealings with the inhabitants of the earth, the "big picture" is extremely important. President Gordon B. Hinkley has warned:

> Sometimes in our day, as we walk our narrow paths and fill our little niches of responsibility, we lose sight of the grand picture . . .

> Some of us do our work as if we had blinders on our eyes. We only see our own little narrow track. We catch nothing of the broader vision. Ours may be a small responsibility in the church. It is good to fulfill that responsibility with diligence. And it is also good to know how that responsibility contributes to the great overall program of the growing kingdom of God.

> Each of us has a small field to cultivate. While so doing, we must never lose sight of the greater picture, the large composite of the divine destiny of this work. It was given us by God our Eternal Father, and each of us has a part to play in the weaving of its magnificent tapestry.

> If each of us does not do well that which is his or hers to do, then there is a flaw in the entire pattern. The whole tapestry is injured. But if each of us does well his or her part, then there is strength and beauty.

The vision of this kingdom is not a superficial dream in the night that fades with sunrise. It is veritably the plan and work of God our Eternal Father. It has to do with all of His children. (*Ensign*, Nov. 1989, pp. 52-54)

As you come to an understanding of the role of the House of Israel in accomplishing the Lord's purposes, your vision of your authority as a patriarch to your children and posterity will enlarge. You will realize the Lord has granted you the same power and authority to bless your seed as he did Abraham.

Teach Your Children to be True to Their Name

A family name is the accumulation of the life and deeds of many people. Family names can be known for both good or bad. Your resolve should be that your children will take pride in their family name. You should encourage them to avoid doing things that would tarnish the respect their forefathers may have earned for their family name.

In instances when children are named after someone in the family, follow Helaman's example and teach your children regarding the significance of their name:

> Behold, my sons, I desire that ye should remember to keep the commandments of God; and I would that ye should declare unto the people these words. Behold, I have given unto you the names of our first parents who came out of the land of Jerusalem; and this I have done that when you remember your names ye may remember them; and when ye remember them ye may remember their works; and when ye remember their works ye may know how that it is said, and also written, that they were good. (Helaman 5:6)

As you successfully teach your children to honor their name, they will have the strength of character to say "no" to things that might lead to their spiritual downfall.

Teach Your Children the Language of Their Forefathers

King Benjamin made certain his children were taught the language of their forefathers. He realized that if his sons did not know the meaning of key words, images, allusions, etc., used in their family records, their ability to understand the writings of their forefathers would be limited (see Mosiah 1:2). The statement that he "caused that they [his children] should be taught the language of his fathers" also suggests that in those instances when the first language in the home is different from the language spoken by the forefathers, fathers may encourage their children to learn that language.

Teach Your Children to Return What They Borrow

Another practical lesson King Benjamin taught his children was to always return things they borrowed (see Mosiah 14:28). So often, hard feelings result when one child borrows something from another member of the family and fails to return it. Teaching your children to return things they borrow is an excellent vehicle to teach them to be responsible. It is a good policy to be strict in holding your children responsible to return money they borrow. This expectation applies to both family members and friends, and especially to money they borrow from you. You will do your children a real disservice if you loan them money to "tide them over" and then not hold them responsible to repay you. This is a common error of many parents. Whether you can afford to give your children the money is not the issue. The critical issue, in character development, is teaching children to return things they borrow, including money borrowed from parents.

Teach Your Children to Find Satisfaction in Work

Unless you as a patriarch assume the responsibility to teach your children to enjoy work in their youth, you risk their going into adulthood not knowing how to work. When this happens, your children will be at a disadvantage. Good work habits are difficult to cultivate later in life.

The following remarks made by Elder L. Tom Perry represent the philosophy of the church on your responsibility to teach your children to work:

> I believe that second only to ensuring that every child receives an understanding of the gospel of our Lord and Savior is teaching them the joy of honest labor.

> Teaching children the joy of honest labor is one of the greatest of all gifts you can bestow upon them. I am convinced that one of the reasons for the breakup of so many couples today is the failure of parents to teach and train sons in their responsibility to provide and care for their families and to enjoy the challenge this responsibility brings. Many of us also have fallen short in instilling within our daughters the desire of bringing beauty and order into their home through homemaking.

> Oh, how essential it is that children be taught early in life the joy that comes from starting and fashioning a job that is the workmanship of their own hands. Teach children the joy of honest labor. Provide a foundation for life that builds confidence and fulfillment in life. "Happy is the man who has work he loves to do. . . . Happy is the man who loves the work he has to do" . . .

> Work is something more than the final end result. It is a discipline. We must learn to do and do well, before we can expect to receive tangible rewards for our labor.

> Let us also teach our children to see that the work assigned is carried to its completion, to take pride in what they accomplish. There is a real satisfaction that comes from finishing a task, especially when it is the best work we know how to do.

> These lessons instilled in me a joy and appreciation for honest labor and prepared me for that time in my life when I would have the responsibility of providing

for a family. The principles I was taught by my wise father of honest labor, of not wasting, of discipline, and of seeing a task to its completion were basic to my success in any profession I might choose to follow. These lessons placed me in a position to face with confidence the challenges of an ever-changing world. (*Ensign*, Nov. 1986, pp. 62-64)

Many critical lessons are to be learned from work. The most obvious are things like learning to manage time, learning to keep records, learning to pay an honest tithe, learning to manage and save money. Children can learn many other lessons if they are required to work in their youth. If your children grow up not having learned these critical lessons, they will experience many frustrations in later life, especially in marriage. Happiness in marriage depends on many of the lessons learned primarily through work.

Teach Your Children to Sing the Hymns of the Church

Make it a practice to sing church hymns in your home, especially during home evenings. In speaking about home evenings, President Ezra Taft Benson said:

Designed to strengthen and safeguard the family, the Church family home evening, one night each week, is to be set apart for fathers and mothers to gather their sons and daughters around them in the home. Prayer is offered, hymns and others songs are sung, scripture is read, family topics are discussed, talent is displayed, principles of the gospel are taught, and often games are played and homemade refreshments served. (*God, Family, Country*, p. 228)

The Lord has revealed his sentiment about songs of worship:

For my soul delighteth in the song of the heart; yea, the song of the righteous is a prayer unto me, and it shall be answered with a blessing upon their heads. (*D&C* 25:12)

112

• • •

And it came to pass that they did break forth, all as
one, in singing, and praising their God for the great
thing which he had done for them, in preserving
them from falling into the hands of their enemies. (3
Nephi 4:31)

The First Presidency has said the following about the
importance of singing church hymns in the home:

Music has boundless powers for moving families
toward greater spirituality and devotion to the gospel.
Latter-day Saints should fill their homes with the
sound of worthy music.

Ours is a hymnbook for the home as well as for the
meetinghouse. We hope the hymnbook will take a
prominent place among the scriptures and other reli-
gious books in our homes. The hymns can bring families a spirit of beauty and peace and can inspire love
and unity among family members.

Teach your children to love the hymns. Sing them as
you work, as you play, and as you travel together. Sing
hymns as lullabies to build faith and testimony in
your young ones.

In addition to blessing us as Church and family members, the hymns can greatly benefit us as individuals.
Hymns can lift our spirits, give us courage, and move
us to righteous action. They can fill our souls with
heavenly thought and bring us a spirit of peace.

Hymns can also help us withstand the temptations of
the adversary. We encourage you to memorize your
favorite hymns and study the scriptures that relate to
them. Then, if unworthy thoughts enter your mind,
sing a hymn to yourself, crowding out the evil with
the good.

Brothers and sisters, let us use the hymns to invite
the spirit of the Lord into our congregations, our
homes, and our personal lives. Let us memorize and

> ponder them, recite and sing them, and partake of their spiritual nourishment. Know that the song of the righteous is a prayer unto our Father in Heaven, "and it shall be answered with a blessing upon [your] heads." (The First Presidency, *Hymns* of the Church of Jesus Christ of Latter-day Saints, p. x)

As your children learn to sing the church hymns and make it a practice to participate when hymns are sung at church meetings, they will be more receptive to the promptings of the spirit.

Help Your Children Find Meaning in Their Personal Prayers

As a patriarch you have several responsibilities with respect to prayer. First and foremost you should take the lead in calling your family together for family prayer and designate who offers the prayer. From your example in offering family prayers and praying with your children on other occasions, your children will learn to pray. As a father you have the responsibility to ensure that your children maintain a pattern of offering their personal prayers regularly. Make it a practice in interviews to ask your children about their personal prayers. Do not assume they are praying. You are responsible to know if your children are praying regularly, infrequently, or not at all.

Through the prophet Joseph Smith the Lord has been very specific in commanding parents to teach their children to pray (see *D&C* 68:28). For the most part, your children will learn to pray by hearing you and your wife pray and by their taking turns in offering family prayer. Children not learning to pray is one of the hazards of not having regular family prayer.

You are responsible to help your children see the need for regular personal prayer, in addition to participation in family prayer. Repeatedly in the scriptures, the Lord instructs us to pray morning and night—as well as in our heart at all times.

Use the following scripture to teach your children about the various forms of prayer:

> And again, I command thee that thou shalt pray vocally as well as in thy heart; yea, before the world as well as in secret, in public as well as in private. (D&C 19:28)

Children need to understand that in addition to the kneeling prayers they offer in the privacy of their room, they need to make it a practice to pray in their minds on various occasions during the day. Help them to realize that if their righteous desires are intense enough, the Lord will view your subconscious thoughts as prayers. This explains how it is possible to pray continually. One of the greatest temptations your children will face is the temptation not to pray. Your children need to be told that Satan will teach them not to pray (see 2 Nephi 32:8). Strive to inspire your children to trust the Lord's promise that the spirit will teach them to pray correctly if their desires are sincere (3 Nephi 19:24; D&C 50:29-30).

In the prayers you offer, avoid vain repetitions (using the same phrases). Stress this point as well when you teach your children about prayer. Above all else, stress the importance of praying frequently, and praying about every facet of their lives (i.e., school, social, family relations), always remembering to express thanks for their blessings.

A statement by President Spencer W. Kimball may help you resolve to enable your children to find meaning in their personal prayers:

> Prayer is an armor of protection against temptation and I promise you that if you will teach your children to pray, fervently and full of faith, many of your problems are solved before they begin. (*Teachings of Spencer W. Kimball*, p. 117)

Help Your Children Understand Sexual Morality

In an effort to teach children about sexual morality, most fathers focus on fornication and say very little about lasciviousness. From the scriptures we learn that the Lord speaks out against both lasciviousness and fornication. The teachings of Jacob are typical:

> And now I, Jacob, spake many more things unto the people of Nephi, warning them against fornication and lasciviousness, and every kind of sin, telling them the awful consequences of them. (Jacob 3:12)

President Spencer W. Kimball spoke out against sexual permissiveness:

> We need to constantly guard against immorality, pornography, and sexual permissiveness that would destroy the purity of the family members, young and old.

> Such evils are very real and very threatening. One has but to read the headlines of our newspapers and magazines to become frighteningly aware of the crumbling, destructive influences which surround us.

> If we could but suggest you go home and lock these evil out by closing and bolting the windows and locking the doors of your homes securely, it would be a simple matter.

> However, such security would be ineffective against the evils which we speak. They come into our homes on ether waves by radio and the television screen. We find these evil forces almost everywhere we go. Exposure is almost constant. We track them into the home from the school, from the playground, from the theater, the office, and the marketplace. There are but few places we go in our everyday world where we can escape them.

> As we have said on previous occasions, certainly our Heavenly Father is distressed with the increasing inroads among his children of such insidious sins as adultery and fornication and homosexuality, lesbianism, abortion . . . (*Ensign*, May 1979, pp. 5-6)

Children need to be taught that any form of lasciviousness is a serious sin (see Alma 45:12). They need to realize that things which cause them to be sexually aroused (i.e., movies, videos, magazines and novels that are suggestive, obscene, or pornographic, vulgar stories, improper thoughts, masturbation, passionate kissing, necking, petting) are forms of lasciviousness. Teach your children that when the Lord commanded "Thou shalt not commit fornication, . . . nor do anything like unto it" (D&C 59:6), he was referring to all forms of lasciviousness. President Ezra Taft Benson has warned:

> Whatever increases the authority of the body over the mind, that thing is a sin to you, however innocent it may seem in itself. (Conference Report, *Improvement Era*, Oct. 1964, p. 67)

• • •

> No sin is causing the loss of the Spirit of the Lord among our people more today than sexual promiscuity. It is causing our people to stumble, damning their growth, hardening their spiritual powers, and making them subject to other sins. (*God, Family, Country*, pp. 239-40)

As a father you need to go to great lengths to help your children understand what is meant by the Lord's commandment that we not commit fornication, "nor do anything like unto it" (D&C 59:6). They need to understand that there are no circumstances that would cause the Lord to condone any degree of passion or sexual arousal outside of marriage.

Satan would like your children to believe that sexual stimulation other than fornication is not a serious sin. He knows that if he can get them to believe this one lie, he can destroy them, no matter how righteous they are in any other respect. Satan knows full well that if he can get your children to embrace any form of lasciviousness, in time they will be consumed with lust. When this happens, children lose their ability to discern between right and wrong. Forms of lasciviousness like masturbation and necking can lead to more serious moral transgressions.

Sexual sins that can jeopardize a person's membership in the church are always preceded by some form of lasciviousness. Your resolve should be to get your children to realize that every kind of sexual exploit (mental, verbal, and physical) resulting in lust or passion is sinful. You need to be very forthright in warning your children that if they choose to become involved in lasciviousness, in any manner, they will "dwindle in unbelief and fall into works of darkness . . . and all manner of iniquities" unless they repent (Alma 45:12).

Encourage your children to look to the example of the Nephites following the Savior's visitation:

> And it came to pass that there was no contention in the land, because of the love of God which did dwell in the hearts of the people.

> And there were no envyings, nor strifes, nor tumults, nor whoredoms, nor lyings, nor murders, nor any manner of lasciviousness; and surely there could not be a happier people among all the people who had been created by the hand of God. (4 Nephi 1:15-16)

Be bold in promising your children that as they will keep themselves free from all forms of lasciviousness, in time the Lord will provide them with wholesome dating relationships and an opportunity to marry a worthy companion in the temple.

Your Children Will Delight in Righteous Living

Resolve to follow Nephi's example in teaching your children: talk of Christ, rejoice in Christ, preach of Christ, prophesy of Christ, write according to the prophecies that your "children may know to what source they may look for a remission of sin" (2 Nephi 25:26). As you are successful in helping your children develop convictions regarding the precepts of the gospel of Jesus Christ, they will be stable. Their lives will be governed substantially by their inner convictions, not an intellectual understanding of right or wrong or what they think is best. Helaman summarizes this promise to his sons:

And now, my sons, remember, remember that it is upon the rock of our Redeemer, who is Christ, the son of God, that ye must build your foundation; that when the devil shall send forth his mighty winds, yea, his shafts in the whirlwind, yea, when all his hail and his mighty storm shall beat upon you, it shall have no power over you to drag you down to the gulf of misery and endless wo, because of the rock upon which ye are built, which is a sure foundation, a foundation whereon if men build they cannot fall. (Helaman 5:12)

In contrast, if your children participate in the church and yet fail to live by gospel precepts, in time they will become very unstable. The Lord has warned: "A double minded [hypocritical] man is unstable in all his ways" (James 1:8). As your children's lives are governed by appropriate convictions, they will refrain from thoughts, language and deeds that are offensive to the Lord. When this proves to be the case, your children will be blessed with good judgment and their mistakes will be minimal. But more important, they will be happy and will delight in righteous living.

8

Write For the Benefit
of Your Children

A misconception has developed in our modern-day society. Many fathers mistakenly believe that it is a mother's responsibility to write the children who are away from home. Mothers should write their children, but this does not excuse a father of his patriarchal duty to write them. When your children are away from home for any reason (missions, school, military), write them on a regular basis. As a patriarch, you have the responsibility to admonish, teach, bless, etc., when you write your children.

Mormon's Two Letters

The Lord illustrated the role of a father as a patriarch by inspiring Moroni to include in the Book of Mormon two letters his father wrote him (see Moroni 8 and 9). These two letters depict Mormon doing several things as a patriarch: teaching, admonishing, blessing, expressing desires, encouraging and testifying.

Moroni explains that the one letter from his father "was written unto me soon after my calling to the ministry" (Moroni 8:1). In the letter, Mormon tells Moroni that he "rejoices exceedingly that [the] Lord Jesus Christ hath been mindful of [him], and hath called [him] to the ministry of his holy work" (Moroni 8:2). Mormon then goes on to tell Moroni that he has been praying in his behalf:

> I am mindful of you always in my prayers, continually praying unto God the Father in the name of his Holy Child, Jesus, that he, through his infinite goodness and grace, will keep you through the endurance of faith on his name to the end. (Moroni 8:3)

It appears that Mormon's letter responds to something Moroni has mentioned in one of his letters to his father. Mormon indicates awareness of disputations between Moroni and others concerning the baptism of little children:

> For, if I have learned the truth, there have been disputations among you concerning the baptism of your little children. (Moroni 8:5)

He then explains why he is writing the letter:

> And now, my son, I desire that ye should labor diligently, that this gross error should be removed from among you; for, for this intent I have written this epistle. (Moroni 8:6)

Mormon tells Moroni that he inquired of the Lord concerning the problem. Then he quotes in his letter the revelation he received from the Lord on the matter:

> Listen to the words of Christ, your Redeemer, your Lord and your God. Behold, I came into the world not to call the righteous but sinners to repentance; the whole need no physician, but they that are sick; wherefore, little children are whole, for they are not capable of committing sin; wherefore the curse of Adam is taken from them in me, that it hath no power over them; and the law of circumcision is done away in me. (Moroni 8:8)

Mormon writes, "After this manner did the Holy Ghost manifest the word of God unto me; wherefore, my beloved son, I know that it is solemn mockery before God, that ye should baptize little children" (Moroni 8:9). In the next several verses he explains the doctrines associated with baptism (see Moroni 8:10-26). It is interesting to note that in the letter, Mormon expresses his intent to write his son again (see Moroni 8:27, 30).

Any son would be touched to learn in a letter from his father that his father is praying continually in his behalf, and has even received a revelation in his behalf. That Moroni felt inclined to include this particular letter in the Book of Mormon suggests it had a profound influence on him.

In Mormon's second letter he tells Moroni of the death of some close acquaintances. He comments on his efforts in calling the Nephites to repentance. He expresses his fear that they will be destroyed by the Lamanites if they do not repent. Here are his words that describe the attitude of the Nephites:

> For so exceedingly do they anger that it seemeth me that they have no fear of death; and they have lost their love, one towards another; and they thirst after blood and revenge continually. (Moroni 9:5)

• • •

> And now, my son, I dwell no longer upon this horrible scene. Behold, thou knowest the wickedness of this people; thou knowest that they are without principle, and past feeling; and their wickedness doth exceed that of the Lamanites. (Moroni 9:20)

Mormon gives his son Moroni some profound counsel:

> And now, my beloved son, notwithstanding their hardness, let us labor diligently; for if we should cease to labor, we should be brought under condemnation; for we have a labor to perform whilst in this tabernacle of clay, that we may conquer the enemy of all righteousness, and rest our souls in the kingdom of God. (Moroni 9:6)

Much of the letter consists of Mormon telling Moroni about the suffering of the Nephites. He relates some of the atrocities which the Nephite women and children have been subjected to at the hands of the Lamanites. Then he goes on to explain that some of the Nephites are guilty of even worse atrocities in torturing the Lamanites (see Moroni 9:7-19).

At one point in the letter, Mormon expresses his confidence in Moroni and prays that the Lord will spare his life.

> Behold, my son, I cannot recommend them unto God lest he should smite me.
>
> But behold, my son, I recommend thee unto God, and I trust in Christ that thou wilt be saved; and I pray unto God that he will spare thy life, to witness the return of his people unto him, or their utter destruction; for I know that they must perish except they repent and return unto him. (Moroni 9:21-22)

Mormon indicates in the letter that he has some sacred records he wants to deliver up to Moroni (see Moroni 9:24). Then, in conclusion, he expresses his hope that this letter will not "weigh [him] down," and he pronounces a blessing upon Moroni:

> My son, be faithful in Christ; and may not the things which I have written grieve thee, to weigh thee down unto death; but may Christ lift thee up, and may his sufferings and death, and the showing his body unto our fathers, and his mercy and long-suffering, and the hope of his glory and of eternal life, rest in your mind forever.
>
> And may the grace of God the Father, whose throne is high in the heavens, and our Lord Jesus Christ who sitteth on the right hand of his power, until all things shall become subject unto him, be, and abide with you forever. Amen. (Moroni 9:25-26)

When you read Moroni's two patriarchal letters, these two chapters in the Book of Moroni take on a great deal of significance. Clearly many of your responsibilities as a patriarch can be accomplished effectively in letters. Study Mormon's letters to his son with a desire to understand more fully your stewardship when you write your own children. A special spirit will accompany your letters if you write them in the spirit of love, especially if you will write your children as a patriarch.

Do Not Limit Your Writing to Letters

The Book of Moroni teaches another very important lesson regarding a father's responsibility as a patriarch. As you read Moroni 7, you will realize that Mormon had recorded some of the talks he had given during his lifetime. Otherwise, Moroni would not have been able to quote his father so extensively. The same holds true for Nephi and other Book of Mormon prophets. If their fathers had not taken the time to record their sermons, experiences, and others' counsel, they would not have been able to include the specific teachings of their fathers in their own writings. By writing extensively to benefit their children, Mormon and other Book of Mormon patriarchs not only reinforced their teachings to their children, they were able to influence their posterity as well. The following are two examples:

> And many more things did king Benjamin write for his sons, which are not written in this book. (Mosiah 1:8)

• • •

> And it came to pass that these were the words which Helaman taught to his sons; yea, he did teach them many things which are not written, and also many things which are written. (Helaman 5:13)

It would be interesting to know exactly how much Lehi wrote for the learning and benefit of his children between the time he experienced his first vision and the time he died. From the following statements of Nephi, we know he wrote a great deal:

> And now, I, Nephi, do not make a full account of the things which my father hath written, for he hath written many things which he saw in visions and in dreams; and he also hath written many things which he prophesied and spake unto his children, of which I shall not make a full account. (1 Nephi 1:16)

• • •

> And all these things did my father see, and hear, and speak, as he dwelt in a tent, in the valley of Lemuel, and also a great many more things, which cannot be written upon these plates. (1 Nephi 9:1)

You have the responsibility to express your feelings about the gospel, share faith-promoting experiences, etc. with your children in writing, in addition to teaching them the gospel of Jesus Christ in family home evenings. This pattern was established anciently, "For a book of remembrance we have written among us, according to the pattern given by the finger of God; and it is given in our own language" (Moses 6:46). Nephi said, "I write the things of my soul . . . for the learning and profit of my children" (2 Nephi 4:15). Jacob explained that it was very difficult to engrave on the plates (see Jacob 4:1). But he went on to say he rejoiced in the labor of writing upon the plates for the benefit of his children; and he expressed the hope that his "children will receive them with thankful hearts, and look upon them that they may learn with joy . . . concerning their . . . parents" (Jacob 4:3). In our day and age, this can be done in writing or on tapes.

In some respects talks and lessons given by a father are of greater consequence in the lives of his children than talks given by church leaders. A father's talk at a son's mission farewell will have a profound influence on the young man, especially if the father speaks as a patriarch to his son.

In various ways, you as a patriarch can write for the benefit of your children. You can keep a personal diary, you can write your life history, you can share with your children outlines of talks and lessons you have given in various church meetings. You can tape record talks and lessons you have given and have copies made for your children. You can make it a practice to write out your testimony once a year and give each of your children a copy. Poems and songs written by you about your children are things your children will treasure. Such efforts to express yourself in writing to your children do not have to be polished; it is the sentiment that counts. If your motives are pure in expressing yourself for the benefit of your children, the Lord will sustain your efforts.

The benefits of what you say when you speak as a patriarch to your children will be enhanced if your remarks are written down. Make it a practice, following blessings and ordinations, to summarize in writing what you say, then give a copy of your notes to your children. It is a wise father who records notes on the blessing he pronounces when he names a child, and who, when the child is old enough, discusses the notes with the child.

The intent of the Lord's commandment to maintain family records is to bless your immediate family, as well as your posterity. For some reason, many fathers lose sight of the power of family records to bless their children at the very time they are written as well as in later years. Consistently look for ways to use your family records for the benefit of your children. For example, if family records are used wisely your children will be better readers (Moses 6:6).

Be Selective in What You Write

You should follow Nephi's standard in determining those things to include in your writings:

> And it matterth not to me that I am particular to give a full account of all the things of my father, for they cannot be written upon these plates, for I desire the room that I may write of the things of God.

> For the fulness of mine intent is that I may persuade men to come unto the God of Abraham, and the God of Isaac, and the God of Jacob, and be saved.

> Wherefore, the things which are pleasing unto the world I do not write, but the things which are pleasing unto God and unto those who are not of the world.

> Wherefore, I shall give commandment unto my seed, that they shall not occupy these plates with things which are not of worth unto the children of men. (1 Nephi 6:3-6)

If you do not have a righteous intent when you write for your children, there is the danger that your writing will not strengthen your children.

The Power of the Holy Ghost Will Magnify Your Writings

It is a real compliment when children say their father was a good man who taught them the gospel of Jesus Christ when they were growing up. However, it is a much greater compliment if they, like Nephi, quote their father extensively in their efforts to teach their own children the gospel of Jesus Christ. If your children have to rely on your verbal teachings, they will not likely quote you very extensively in their efforts to teach their own children the gospel.

In contrast, if you make it a practice to write for the benefit of your children throughout your life, your children will be inclined to quote you in the same way Nephi and Moroni quoted their fathers. In addition, if you have recorded your teachings, testimony, etc., your grandchildren and great-grandchildren can be blessed directly from your writing as well. Make it a practice to devote some time each Sunday to writing for the benefit of your children. You will discover that as you make it a practice to study and ponder the scriptures, the Lord will magnify you in your efforts to express yourself in writing to your children (see 2 Nephi 4:14-16). The Lord has promised fathers will be inspired in their efforts to write for the benefit of their children:

> And a book of remembrance was kept, in the which was recorded, in the language of Adam, for it was given unto as many as called upon God to write by the spirit of inspiration. (Moses 6:5)

Even though Mormon, Lehi, and other Book of Mormon fathers did not enjoy our modern-day conveniences for writing, they still found time to write extensively for the benefit of their children. As you read the writings of their sons, it is very evident that the writings of their fathers profoundly influenced them. Strive to emulate their example by sharing your teachings, faith-promoting experiences, etc. with your children in writing, or on tapes. Be assured that no matter how limited you are in expressing yourself, through the power of the Holy Ghost your writings "will be made strong . . ." unto your children and ". . . persuadeth them to do good; and maketh known unto them of their fathers and [they] . . . speaketh of Jesus, and persuadeth them to believe in him, and to endure to the end, which is life eternal" (see 2 Nephi 33:1-4).

9

Fast and Pray
For Your Children

One of your major responsibilities as a patriarch is to pray with and in behalf of your children. When the Savior was instructing the Nephites on prayer, he instructed fathers to pray with their wives and children:

> Pray in your families unto the Father, always in my name, that your wives and your children may be blessed. (3 Nephi 18:21)

At a minimum you should assemble your family for prayer at least once a day. Ideally you should pray morning and night with your family. Commenting on home worship, President Spencer W. Kimball said:

> Our Father in Heaven has given us the blessing of prayer to help us succeed in our all-important activities of home and life. I know that if we pray fervently and righteously, individually and as a family, when we arise in the morning and when we retire at night, and around our tables at mealtime, we will not only knit together as loved ones but we will grow spiritually. We have so much need for our Heavenly Father's help as we seek to learn gospel truths and then live

them, and as we seek his help in the decisions of our lives. It is especially in our family circles where our children can learn how to talk to Heavenly Father by listening to their parents. They can learn about heartfelt and honest prayer from such experiences.

In the family prayer there is even more than the supplication and prayer of gratitude. It is a forward step toward family unity and family solidarity. It builds family consciousness and establishes a spirit of family interdependence. Here is a moment of the rushed day with blatant radios hushed, lights low, and all minds and hearts turned to each other and to the infinite; a moment when the world is shut out and heaven enclosed within. (*Teachings of Spencer W. Kimball*, p. 116)

Family Prayer

When you are at home, you are responsible to take charge and call on someone to offer the family prayer. It is not proper for you to do all the praying. Every member of your family should have his or her turn. In your absence, your wife is in charge. If you are both gone your oldest child is in charge. Strive to be on your knees as a family every day, praying to the Lord.

The focus of your family prayers should be expressions of thanks and gratitude. You should pray for church leaders, including your local bishop. You should pray for your own family members, "their incomings and outgoings, their travels, their work, and all pertaining to them. When children pray audibly for their brothers and sisters, it is likely that quarreling and conflicts and jarrings will be lessened" (*Teachings of Spencer W. Kimball*, p. 121). You should pray for enlightenment and forgiveness. In speaking about what you should pray for, President Kimball said, "We pray for everything that is needed and dignified and proper" (*Teachings of Spencer W. Kimball*, p. 122).

Family prayer is a good teaching setting. As your children hear you express your love for Deity in your prayers, their love for God will increase. As your children hear you express your dependence on the Lord, they will learn to look to the Lord.

Teach your children that "the family prayer should be in length and composition appropriate to the need. . . . One can do much thanking and requesting in one or two minutes, though there are obviously times when it might be appropriate to commune longer" (*Teachings of Spencer W. Kimball*, p. 119).

Commenting further on prayer, President Kimball gave some very candid counsel:

> How often do we hear people who wax eloquent in their prayers to the extent of preaching a complete sermon? The hearers tire and the effect is lost, and I sometimes wonder if perhaps the dial of the heavenly radio is not turned off when long and wordy prayers are sent heavenward. I feel sure that there is too much to do in heaven for the Lord and his servants to sit indefinitely listening to verbose praises and requests. (*Teachings of Spencer W. Kimball*, pp. 119-120)

He also cautioned:

> There may be those who pray for certain blessings without any question in their minds as to the value of those things to them. Perhaps they are disappointed and even shaken in their faith if their prayer is not granted. Remember that our prayers are often as inconsistent and inappropriate to our Father in Heaven as are the demands of our little children upon us. (*Teachings of Spencer W. Kimball*, p. 123)

Be assured that as your children are consistently prayerful while growing up, they will become acquainted with the Lord and will be disposed to look to Him for guidance throughout their lives.

Be Bold in Pronouncing Blessings in Behalf of Your Family

Be bold in pronouncing blessings in behalf of your family when you offer prayers in their presence. As a patriarch you

133

have the authority to pronounce blessings as the spirit directs you, instead of merely praying for blessings. The right to pronounce blessings illustrates, as much as anything else, the authority a righteous father has as a patriarch.

Pray Continually for Your Children

Follow Nephi's example. He prayed continually for his children during the day and wept for them in prayer in the evenings. He maintained an attitude of faith that the Lord would answer his prayers: "I know that the Lord God will consecrate my prayers for the gain of my people" (see 2 Nephi 33:3-4).

Between the time you arise in the morning and retire at night, there are numerous occasions when you can pray in behalf of your children. You have the time you spend getting ready in the morning and the time you spend traveling to and from work, in addition to many other moments during the day when your mind is free to pray.

Learn to Pray More Effectively

The teachings of Amulek to the Zoramites can assist you in your efforts to learn to pray more effectively.

> Therefore may God grant unto you, my brethren, that ye may begin to exercise your faith unto repentance, that ye begin to call upon his holy name, that he would have mercy upon you;
>
> Yea, cry unto him for mercy; for he is mighty to save.
>
> Yea, humble yourselves, and continue in prayer unto him.
>
> Cry unto him when ye are in your fields, yea, over all your flocks.
>
> Cry unto him in your houses, yea, over all your household, both morning, mid-day, and evening.
>
> Yea, cry unto him against the power of your enemies.
>
> Yea, cry unto him against the devil, who is an enemy to all righteousness.

Cry unto him over the crops of your fields, that ye may prosper in them.

Cry over the flocks of your fields, that they may increase.

But this is not all; ye must pour out your souls in your closets, and your secret places, and in your wilderness.

Yea, and when you do not cry unto the Lord, let your hearts be full, drawn out in prayer unto him continually for your welfare, and also for the welfare of those who are around you.

And now behold, my beloved brethren, I say unto you, do not suppose that this is all; for after ye have done all these things, if ye turn away the needy, and the naked, and visit not the sick and afflicted, and impart of your substance, if ye have, to those who stand in need—I say unto you, if ye do not any of these things, behold, your prayer is vain, and availeth you nothing, and ye are as hypocrites who do deny the faith. (Alma 34:17-28)

Several important concepts regarding your responsibility as a patriarch are taught in these verses:

- *Pray that the Lord will bless your family.*
- *Be disposed to pray many times, both inside and outside your home, regarding your family.*
- *Pray in the home morning, midday and evening.*
- *Pray to the Lord regarding the enemies of your family, such as people who make your wife or children unhappy (i.e., classmates, certain teachers).*
- *Pray that your children will be protected from the devil.*
- *Pray regarding your employment or livelihood, with the desire to increase your earning power.*
- *Pray secretly as well as with your family.*
- *In addition to prayers you offer when you are kneeling, learn to pray in behalf of your family when you are driving, jogging, etc.*

135

- *Remember the Lord's warning that unless you are effective as a home teacher, pay a generous fast offering, etc., your prayers in behalf of your family will be vain and will avail them nothing.*

You can learn a lot about prayer from a careful study of the prayer Nephi recorded (see 2 Nephi 4:16-35). It is interesting to note that he speaks to himself as well as to the Lord. You will find it a constructive exercise to occasionally review your personal prayers in light of this example.

Look to the Savior's Example

In speaking of prayer, Jesus instructs us to pray even as he prayed among the Nephites (see 3 Nephi 18:16). You should make a careful study of the Savior's ministry among the Nephites in your effort to enhance the power of your personal prayers.

Even though the Savior was only with the Nephites for a short while, he emphasized prayer. He clarified the prayers associated with baptism, the sacrament, and the receipt of the Holy Ghost. He instructed the Nephites extensively regarding personal prayers (3 Nephi 13:58; 3 Nephi 14:7-11; 3 Nephi 17:15-23). He instructed them to pray for understanding (3 Nephi 17:3). He prayed for them (3 Nephi 17:13-17). He prayed for their children (3 Nephi 17:21). He taught them to pray unto the Father in His name (3 Nephi 19:16). He taught them to seek the gift of the Holy Ghost through prayer (3 Nephi 19:9). He commanded those he had designated as leaders to pray for the people while he prayed in their behalf (3 Nephi 19:16-17).

The following verses illustrate Jesus' emphasis on prayer when He taught the Nephites:

And the twelve did teach the multitude; and behold, they did cause that the multitude should kneel down upon the face of the earth, and should pray unto the Father in the name of Jesus.

And the disciples did pray unto the Father also in the name of Jesus. And it came to pass that they arose and ministered unto the people.

And when they had ministered those same words which Jesus had spoken—nothing varying from the words which Jesus had spoken—behold, they knelt again and prayed to the Father in the name of Jesus.

And they did pray for that which they most desired; and they desired that the Holy Ghost should be given unto them.

And when they had thus prayed they went down unto the water's edge, and the multitude followed them.

And it came to pass that Nephi went down into the water and was baptized.

And he came up out of the water and began to baptize. And he baptized all those whom Jesus had chosen.

And it came to pass when they were all baptized and had come up out of the water, the Holy Ghost did fall upon them, and they were filled with the Holy Ghost and with fire.

And behold, they were encircled about as if it were by fire; and it came down from heaven, and the multitude did witness it, and did bear record; and angels did come down out of heaven and did minister unto them.

And it came to pass that while the angels were ministering unto the disciples, behold, Jesus came and stood in the midst and ministered unto them.

And it came to pass that he spake unto the multitude, and commanded them that they should kneel down again upon the earth, and also that his disciples should kneel down upon the earth.

And it came to pass that when they had all knelt down upon the earth, he commanded his disciples that they should pray.

And behold, they began to pray; and they did pray unto Jesus, calling him their Lord and their God.

And it came to pass that Jesus departed out of the midst of them, and went a little way off from them and bowed himself to the earth, and he said:

Father, I thank thee that thou hast given the Holy Ghost unto these whom I have chosen; and it is because of their belief in me that I have chosen them out of the world.

Father, I pray thee that thou wilt give the Holy Ghost unto all them that shall believe in their words.

Father, thou hast given them the Holy Ghost because they believe in me; and thou seest that they believe in me because thou hearest them, and they pray unto me; and they pray unto me because I am with them.

And now Father, I pray unto thee for them, and also for all those who shall believe in me, that I may be in them as thou, Father, art in me, that we may be one.

And it came to pass that when Jesus had thus prayed unto the Father, he came unto his disciples, and behold, they did still continue, without ceasing, to pray unto him; and they did not multiply many words, for it was given unto them what they should pray, and they were filled with desire.

And it came to pass that Jesus blessed them as they did pray unto him; and his countenance did smile upon them, and the light of his countenance did shine upon them, and behold they were as white as the countenance and also the garments of Jesus; and behold the whiteness thereof did exceed all the whiteness, yea, even there could be nothing upon earth so white as the whiteness thereof.

And Jesus said unto them: Pray on; nevertheless they did not cease to pray.

And he turned from them again and went a little way off and bowed himself to the earth; and he prayed again unto the Father, saying:

Father, I thank thee that thou hast purified those whom I have chosen, because of their faith, I pray for them, and also for them who shall believe on their words, even as they are purified in me.

Father, I pray not for the world, but for those whom thou hast given me out of the world, because of their faith, that they may be purified in me, that I may be in them as thou, Father, art in me, that we may be one, that I may be glorified in them.

And when Jesus had spoken these words he came again unto his disciples; and behold they did pray steadfastly, without ceasing, unto him; and he did smile upon them again; and behold they were white, even as Jesus.

And it came to pass that he went again a little way off and prayed unto the Father;

And tongue cannot speak the words which he prayed, neither can be written by man the words which he prayed.

And the multitude did hear and do bear record; and their hearts were open and they did understand in their hearts the words which he prayed.

Nevertheless, so great and marvelous were the words which he prayed that they cannot be written, neither can they be uttered by man.

And it came to pass that when Jesus had made an end of praying he came again to the disciples, and said unto them: So great faith have I never seen among all the Jews; wherefore I could not show unto them so great miracles, because of their unbelief. (3 Nephi 19:6-35)

From the Savior's example, it is evident that you should pray on many occasions in many different ways with your family. The point is that family prayer and blessings on the food at mealtime are not sufficient. Your goal should be to pray with your family as the spirit directs. Spencer W. Kimball promised that families would be more like the City of Enoch if they were on their knees every night and morning, and if parents prayed for their sons and daughters twice daily (*Teachings of Spencer W. Kimball*, pp. 116-117). If you do not feel the spirit is guiding you in this regard, fast and pray until you feel confident the Lord is guiding you. You will need to trust the Lord to teach you how and when to pray.

Fast With and in Behalf of Your Children

Some problems associated with your children cannot be resolved by prayer alone. This basic lesson is illustrated in the effort of Jesus' disciples to cure a man, as in the New Testament records:

> Lord, have mercy on my son: for he is a lunatic, and sore vexed: for ofttimes he falleth into the fire, and oft into the water.
>
> And I brought him to thy disciples, and they could not cure him.
>
> Then Jesus answered and said, O faithless and perverse generation, how long shall I be with you? How long shall I suffer you? Bring him hither to me.
>
> And Jesus rebuked the devil; and he departed out of him: and the child was cured from that very hour.
>
> Then came the disciples to Jesus apart, and said, Why could not we cast him out?
>
> And Jesus said unto them, Because of your unbelief: for verily I say unto you, If ye have faith as a grain of mustard seed, ye shall say unto this mountain, Remove hence to yonder place; and it shall remove; and nothing shall be impossible unto you.
>
> Howbeit this kind goeth not out but by prayer and fasting. (Matt 17:17-21; see also Mark 9:17-29)

140

It is appropriate to offer to fast with your children as well as fast secretly in their behalf in some instances. Some problems even warrant inviting others who have a concern for the welfare of a child to join in the fast. Alma not only fasted and prayed for his son, he invited others to join him. The following verses refer to Alma's prayers in behalf of his son. They also refer to Alma's later inviting others to join him in fasting and prayer in behalf of his son.

> And again, the angel said: Behold, the Lord hath heard the prayers of his people, and also the prayers of his servant, Alma, who is thy father; for he has prayed with much faith concerning thee that thou mightest be brought to the knowledge of the truth; therefore, for this purpose have I come to convince thee of the power and authority of God, that the prayers of his servants might be answered according to their faith. (Mosiah 27:14)

• • •

> And he caused that the multitude should be gathered together that they might witness what the Lord had done for his son, and also for those that were with him.
>
> And he caused that the priests should assemble themselves together; and they began to fast, and to pray to the Lord their God that he would open the mouth of Alma, that he might speak, and also that his limbs might receive their strength—that the eyes of the people might be opened to see and know of the goodness and glory of God. (Mosiah 27:21-23)

In the 58th chapter of Isaiah the Lord enumerates promises to those who fast conscientiously. He promises specifically that we will be freed from frustrations, and that we will receive the blessing of peace. On some occasions when you fast, your focus should be the welfare of your children. When your children face special challenges, you should follow President Ezra Taft Benson's advice and put their names on the prayer rolls of the temple. Through fasting, your recep-

141

tiveness to inspiration and spiritual guidance will be enhanced as you draw closer to your Heavenly Father.

Earnest Prayer Availeth Much Good

Your children should hear you pray in their behalf at least once a week. When you kneel in family prayer, your children learn habits that will stay with them all through their lives. When your children are away from home for any reason and you communicate with them by mail, let them know you pray in their behalf every day. Then, in later years when you visit your married children, they will invite you to kneel with them for family prayer. Seeing this pattern in the lives of your married children will be a tremendous source of joy for you.

Teach your children that the Lord does not promise freedom from adversity and affliction. As they are taught to appreciate the role of prayer in our lives, they will see it as an avenue of communication that allows us to seek his help and guidance in dealing with challenges. As you make it a practice to follow the teachings of the scriptures and modern-day prophets regarding fasting and prayer, your prayers as a patriarch will avail much good in behalf of your family, especially if you learn to be bold in exercising your authority as a patriarch in pronouncing blessings in their behalf as the spirit directs.

10

Interview Your Children

Even though the term *interview* is not used in the scriptures, several accounts in the Old Testament and Book of Mormon tell of righteous fathers talking to their children individually. In these accounts, the Lord portrays the role of a father as a patriarch interviewing his children. In the truest sense of the word, these ancient patriarchs discharged their responsibility to teach their children individually. Modern-day fathers would be more effective in discharging their responsibility as patriarchs if they would follow the example of ancient patriarchs in their private conversations with their children.

Identify the Individual Needs of Your Children

Make a clear distinction between interviews and casual conversation. The distinguishing characteristic is not where the interview occurs, but that an interview involves prayerful consideration of those things to be discussed. In an interview an insightful father will focus on the special needs and talents of each of his children, realizing that each is unique and should be approached differently. At the same time, realize that you should not attempt to deal with too many issues at one time in an interview. One issue discussed and resolved is much better than many issues discussed with nothing resolved.

During an Interview You Have Several Responsibilities

During an interview with your children, you have the sacred responsibility to give direction, to discuss standards, to help set appropriate goals, and to teach the doctrines of the gospel. Speaking of this sacred responsibility, President Harold B. Lee said,

> In a time we have been told would be much as the days of Noah, we must help young to make right choices, to grow in justified self-esteem, especially when they can be under the direct influence of the home, where family love can make repentance both possible and significant. The environment of our young people outside of the home and church will often be either empty so far as values are concerned or contain ideas that contradict the principles of the gospel. (*Ensign*, March 1971, p. 3)

Interviewing your children can be a powerful means of getting close to them and improving the overall quality of family life in your home. Good things will result when you interview your sons and daughters as a patriarch. If done properly, interviews result in a bond of love between a father and his children. Elder A. Theodore Tuttle explains the importance of this relationship:

> To the extent we become friends with our children in unconditional love, to that extent we become like our Father in Heaven. (*Ensign*, Jan. 1974, p. 67)

If you are sensitive, you will see special things happen when you teach your children during interviews. When you teach all of your children together during family home evenings your children will benefit, but you will discover the benefits are much greater when you teach your children individually.

You will discover that your best effort in teaching your children will not be good enough unless you are willing to interact with your children individually. It is very important that your children have some private time with you regularly. In speaking to fathers in Israel, President Harold B. Lee said, "You teach your family generally, and each child individually the doctrines of the kingdom" (*Father, Consider Your Ways* [Pamphlet, PBCT0496], p. 5).

It is your responsibility to show each of your children personal individual attention. Time spent with individual children is just as important as family activities. Personal time with a father results in children feeling special and important. With planning and commitment, you will be able to interact with your children individually to a much greater extent. Look for opportunities to have your children spend part of a day with you at work. Invite one of your children to go with you to run errands. Work with your children individually in the yard. Invite individual children to join you as you visit neighbors or those who are home-bound. Take a child with you when you will be gone overnight in conjunction with your work or for other purposes. Plan some activities specifically for individual children.

The things you do with your children individually pay the biggest dividends. Material things (i.e., clothes, the family car, the size of the home) do not mold the lives of your children. Time with you is a child's most valuable commodity. If you lose sight of this fundamental truth, you will fail to some degree with your children.

Ask Probing Questions

The Book of Mormon does not depict fathers asking their children questions. However, you can still learn a great deal from the Book of Mormon about asking your children questions. Look to Alma's example (see Alma 5). This chapter includes more probing questions than any other chapter in the Book of Mormon, any one of which (with slight adapta-

145

tions) could be used in a constructive way by you in interviews with your children.

Make Use of the Scriptures

Make it a practice to read and quote selected verses of scriptures to your children during interviews. As your children hear you read and quote the scriptures when you interview them, they will sense that the Lord is speaking to them. In time, your children will know the word of the Lord as it applies to the issues they face in their youth.

From the example of righteous Book of Mormon fathers, we see they used the scriptures extensively when they taught their children. Beginning with father Lehi, the Book of Mormon shows a father using the scriptures to teach his children the gospel of Jesus Christ. Once Lehi had the brass plates, he quoted from them extensively when he taught his children (see 1 Nephi 5:10-22).

Nephi followed his father's example, making it a practice to read and quote from the scriptures when he taught his children (see 1 Nephi 19:22-24). Lehi's younger son, Jacob, also followed his father's example in quoting from the scriptures when he taught the gospel of Jesus Christ (see Jacob 2:23-24; Jacob 4:5-6; Jacob 6:10-13). King Benjamin likewise used the brass plates to teach his children the gospel of Jesus Christ (Mosiah 1:3). We find this same pattern in the writings of Helaman (Helaman 5:9-10).

Great missionaries throughout the Book of Mormon used the scriptures when they taught (e.g., Alma, Amulek, Ammon and the sons of Mosiah). When you read or quote from the Book of Mormon, make your children aware that the Book of Mormon was written specifically to help them meet the challenges of this day and age. Use the remarks of President Benson to help your children understand this point:

> The Book of Mormon was written for us today. God is the author of the Book. It is a record of a fallen people, compiled by inspired men for our blessing today. Those people never had the Book—it was meant for

146

us. Mormon, the ancient prophet after whom the Book was named, abridged centuries of records. God, who knows the end from the beginning, told him what to include in his abridgement that we would need for our day. Mormon turned the records over to his son Moroni, the last recorder; and Moroni wrote over 1500 years ago, but speaking to us today he states, "Behold, I speak unto you as if you were present, and yet ye are not. But behold, Jesus Christ has shown ye unto me. I know your doings. (Moroni 8:35) (*A Witness and a Warning*, p. 2)

As a patriarch you will be negligent if you do not follow the example of these great Book of Mormon fathers and make it a practice to quote and read from the scriptures when you interview your children. Your challenge is to help them realize that the scriptures apply to their life and situation today.

Learn From Lehi's Example

The pattern Lehi followed in his conversation with his children is an excellent guide for you in interviewing your children (see 1 Nephi 8:37-39):

- *First he spoke to his children with all of the feelings of a tender parent, encouraging them to hearken to his words.*

- *Then he promised his children that if they would follow his counsel, the Lord would be merciful unto them.*

- *Then he preached to his children and prophesied in their behalf.*

- *He concluded by once again encouraging his children to keep the commandments.*

If you make it a practice to do these things when you interview your children on a fairly consistent basis, your interviews will be effective.

Your Children Need to Do Their Part

A comparison of Nephi's response to his father's teachings and that of his older brothers should be pointed out to your children fairly frequently. The following verses describe Nephi's reaction to his father's teachings:

> And it came to pass that I, Nephi, being exceeding young, nevertheless being large in stature, and also having great desires to know of the mysteries of God, wherefore, I did cry unto the Lord; and behold he did visit me, and did soften my heart that I did believe all the words which had been spoken by my father; wherefore, I did not rebel against him like unto my brothers.

> And it came to pass after I, Nephi, having heard all the words of my father, concerning the things which he saw in a vision, and also the things which he spake by the power of the Holy Ghost, which power he received by faith on the Son of God—and the Son of God was the Messiah who should come—I, Nephi, was desirous also that I might see, and hear, and know of these things, by the power of the Holy Ghost, which is the gift of God unto all those who diligently seek him, as well in times of old as in the time that he should manifest himself unto the children of men. (1 Nephi 10:17)

• • •

> For it came to pass that after I had desired to know the things that my father had seen, and believing that the Lord was able to make them known unto me, as I sat pondering in mine heart I was caught away in the Spirit of the Lord, yea, into an exceedingly high mountain, which I never had before seen, and upon which I never had before set my foot. (1 Nephi 11:1)

In contrast, his older brothers were not inclined to pray regarding their father's teachings.

> And it came to pass that after I had received strength I spake unto my brethren, desiring to know of them the cause of their disputations.

> And they said: Behold, we cannot understand the words which our father hath spoken concerning the

natural branches of the olive-tree, and also concerning the Gentiles.

And I said unto them: Have ye inquired of the Lord?

And they said unto me: We have not; for the Lord maketh no such thing known unto us. (1 Nephi 15:6-9)

Your children need to realize that unless they are willing to live righteously, they will not be receptive to counsel they receive from you as a patriarch. In the following verses, Nephi explains this basic truth to his older brothers:

And now it came to pass that after I, Nephi, had made an end of speaking to my brethren, behold they said unto me: Thou hast declared unto us hard things, more than we are able to bear.

And it came to pass that I said unto them that I knew that I had spoken hard things against the wicked, according to the truth; and the righteous have I justified, and testified that they should be lifted up at the last day; wherefore, the guilty taketh the truth to be hard, for it cutteth them to the very center.

And now my brethren, if ye were righteous and were willing to hearken to the truth, and give heed unto it, that ye might walk uprightly before God, then ye would not murmur because of the truth, and say: Thou speakest hard things against us.

And it came to pass that I, Nephi, did exhort my brethren, with all diligence, to keep the commandments of the Lord. (1 Nephi 16:1-4).

Show a Genuine Interest

Just as important as teaching and counseling, you should always show a genuine interest in those things your children enjoy, such as sports and hobbies. Make it a practice to praise your children for their accomplishments. More important than anything else, always let your children know they are loved and appreciated. Children need to hear this assurance often. In reference to this critical stewardship, President Ezra Taft Benson said,

> Rearing happy, peaceful children is no easy challenge in today's world, but it can be done, and it is being done. Responsible parenthood is the key. Above all else, children need to know and feel they are loved, wanted, and appreciated. They need to be assured of that often. (*Ensign*, Nov. 1982, p. 60)

Establish an Atmosphere of Open Communication

When you interview your children, attempt to create an atmosphere in which they can express themselves honestly and openly. A loving father will always do everything in his power to keep the lines of communication open with his children. An effective interview results in bond-building communications.

The key to open communication is listening, which means more than just being quiet. It means giving someone your undivided attention. The most important time to listen is when a child needs to be heard. Courtesy and respect on your part are essential. Learn to be very tolerant of the points of view expressed by your children.

Once open lines of communication are established, you may hear your children criticize you. Just as Laman and Lemuel murmured against their father, there may be times when your children will murmur against you. This can be painful, but if you will listen openly and refrain from getting defensive, you can learn a great deal from them. Remember that your children are entitled to inspiration (see Alma 32:23).

Speak as a Patriarch

An interview is an ideal time for you to speak to your children as a patriarch (i.e., counsel, teach, promise blessings, etc.). Approach interviews with the resolve to do and say specific things as a patriarch; then be open to the promptings of the spirit to do and say additional things as you are inspired.

As you make it a practice to speak to your children as a patriarch, their respect for you will be greatly enhanced. When you speak, they will listen. They will have confidence in your opinions and your counsel. As you speak to your children as a patriarch during interviews, your remarks will have a profound influence on them, much more lasting than lessons they receive outside of the home.

Follow the Savior's Example

Use the Savior's example and the scriptures generally as your guides in planning your interviews with your children. Show concern for their progress in "wisdom," which includes school, reading good books, etc. Always attend to their "stature," which involves physical and emotional health, personal appearance, and feelings of self-worth. Discuss their "favor with God," obedience to the commandments, prayers, payment of tithes, testimony, scripture study, and overall spiritual growth. Do not overlook your children's "favor with men." Social development and interpersonal relationships with peers and family members are important (see Luke 2:52).

As your children get older, service and love for their fellowmen should be a point of focus. It is very important that your children learn to be giving and caring; otherwise they will be discontented and unhappy.

Understand Your Role in Relationship to the Role of a Bishop

It is very important that you understand your role in interviewing and counseling your children in relationship to the role of a bishop. Elder Boyd K. Packer has made it very clear—the primary responsibility rests with you:

> Bishops, keep constantly in mind that fathers are responsible to preside over their families. . . . If my boy needs counseling, Bishop, it should be my responsibility first, and yours second. If my boy needs recreation, Bishop, I should provide it first, and you second. If my boy needs correction, that should be my

responsibility first, and yours second. If I am failing as a father, help me first, and my children second. Do not be too quick to take over for me the job of raising my children. Do not be too quick to counsel them and solve all of their problems. Get me involved; it is my ministry. (*Ensign*, May 1978, p. 93)

Attempt to know more about your children's strivings, struggles and concerns than their bishop. When it proves necessary, keep the bishop informed about your children. But never relinquish to a bishop your stewardship of patriarch to your children. If your children confess a serious moral transgression to you, help them understand why they will need to discuss the matter with their bishop. Children need to understand the bishop's role as a judge in Israel.

Basic Guidelines

Some basic guidelines, if followed, will result in effective interviews. Interviews should be simple, informal and relaxed. Avoid anger, accusation, and lectures. Make it a practice to deal with your children's interests first before you address your fatherly concerns. Either open or conclude the interview with a prayer. In those instances when you offer the prayer, pronounce blessings in behalf of your children.

Summarize Points Discussed in Interviews in Writing

From the writings of Lehi and Alma we learn a very important lesson about fathers' interviews. These great patriarchs made it a practice to summarize in writing the points covered in interviews with their children. Otherwise the Book of Mormon would not contain a detailed record of things these prophets said in their interviews with their children.

Keep a record of your children's non-confidential goals and concerns so you don't forget to follow up on critical points, providing positive reinforcement. Written records will make your interviews with your children much more effective.

Have Specific Objectives in Mind

Each time you interview one of your children, have some specific objectives in mind. These may relate to any aspect of a child's life (i.e., savings goals, refraining from fault-finding of others, household chores). However, your overall objective in interviewing your children should be to teach them to serve their fellowmen and to build the kingdom of God here on the earth. If you are successful in teaching these two basic truths, your children will develop line upon line, and precept upon precept. The fruits of the spirit will become very evident in their character. Over the years your children will develop character attributes specified in the scriptures, such as faith, virtue, knowledge, temperance, patience, brotherly kindness, godliness, charity, kindness, diligence, and others.

President Spencer W. Kimball commented on objectives that are realized when fathers are conscientious in interviewing their children:

> While one objective is reached by merely being together, yet the additional and greater value can come from the lessons of life. The father will teach the children. Here they can learn integrity, honor, dependableness, sacrifice, and faith in God. Life's experiences and the scriptures are the basis of the teaching and this, wrapped up in filial and parental love, makes an impact nothing else can make. Thus, reservoirs of righteousness are filled to carry children through the dark days of temptation and desire, of drought and skepticism. (*Teachings of Spencer W. Kimball*, p. 334)

If you fail to perform this critical patriarchal duty of establishing your children on the "strait and narrow way," you run the risk of losing your children to the enticements of the adversary. You just cannot afford not to spend time each month interviewing your children. There is just no substitute for individual time with them. The dividends from interviews demonstrate that proper interviewing is a very wise use of your time—the most productive of any of the time you spend with your children.

11

Dealing With
Wayward Children

A study of the scriptures reveals a harsh reality. In spite of parents' best effort, some children may rebel against the commandments of God. Beginning with Father Adam, even prophets have had rebellious children. In God's great wisdom, the scriptures contain accounts of righteous fathers whose children rejected God's commandments.

If you have children who turn against the commandments, you need to do three things. First, remind yourself that the Lord ordained that we have our free agency in mortality. Second, exercise faith in the power of your teachings to cause your children to see the error in their ways. Third, follow the Lord's example in repeatedly inviting them back.

Your Children are Free to Act for Themselves

Your relationship with your children is just like God's relationship with his children here on earth. You can persuade and direct your children in any number of ways, but you cannot force them to live righteously. They are free to choose good or evil. As the hymn, "Know This, That Every Soul Is Free" expresses so well, you cannot force the human mind. It is free agency that makes it possible for your children to be exalted. It is also the reason they will be held strictly accountable for their sins. Lehi expressed this basic truth very well:

> And the Messiah cometh in the fulness of time, that he may redeem the children of men from the fall. And because that they are redeemed from the fall they have become free forever, knowing good from evil; to act for themselves and not to be acted upon, save it be by the punishment of the law at the great and last day, according to the commandments which God hath given.
>
> Wherefore, men are free according to the flesh; and all things are given them which are expedient unto man. And they are free to choose liberty and eternal life, through the great mediation of all men, or to choose captivity and death, according to the captivity and power of the devil; for he seeketh that all men might be miserable like unto himself.
>
> And now, my sons, I would that ye should look to the great Mediator, and hearken unto his great commandments; and be faithful unto his words, and choose eternal life, according to the will of his Holy Spirit;
>
> And not choose eternal death, according to the will of the flesh and the evil which is therein, which giveth the spirit of the devil power to captivate, to bring you down to hell, that he may reign over you in his own kingdom.
>
> I have spoken these few words unto you all, my sons, in the last days of my probation; and I have chosen the good part, according to the words of the prophet. And I have none other object save it be the everlasting welfare of your souls. (2 Nephi 2:26-30)

Here are the words of a modern-day prophet:

> There is no guarantee, of course, that righteous parents will succeed always in holding their children, and certainly they may lose them if they do not do all

in their power. Children have their free agency.
(*Teachings of Spencer W. Kimball*, p. 335)

If your children did not have their free agency, the purpose of their mortal existence would be lost. They would not be able to experience happiness and would not be able to develop spiritually. If this were the case, your children would not have the opportunity to qualify for eternal life.

Exercise Faith in the Power of Your Teachings

You will err as a father if you get frustrated with the consequences of your children exercising their agency. Remember, Satan sought to destroy the agency of man in the pre-existence and was consequently expelled from the presence of God (see Moses 4:3). Of necessity, your position should be to do everything in your power to persuade your children to live righteously, and then to accept God's plan that they are free to choose how to live. In some instances, children will choose to break God's commandments. When they do, you need to exercise faith that, at some point in time, your previous teachings will prompt them to repent.

The writings of Enos are an excellent example of the powerful influence a father's teachings can have on his children:

> Behold, it came to pass that I, Enos, knowing my father that he was a just man—for he taught me in his language, and also in the nurture and admonition of the Lord and blessed be the name of my God for it—
>
> And I will tell you of the wrestle which I had before God, before I received a remission of my sins.
>
> Behold, I went to hunt beasts in the forests; and the words which I had often heard my father speak concerning eternal life, and the joy of the saints, sunk deep into my heart.
>
> And my soul hungered; and I kneeled down before my Maker, and I cried unto him in mighty prayer and supplication for mine own soul; and all the day long

did I cry unto him; yea, and when the night came I
did still raise my voice high that it reached the heavens.

And there came a voice unto me, saying: Enos, thy
sins are forgiven thee, and thou shalt be blessed.
(Enos 1-5)

We are not provided with specifics, but it appears that
Enos' father was dead, yet his words were still a key factor in
Enos' motivation to seek the Lord.

Another example of the influence of a father's teachings on
his children is the miraculous conversion of Alma the
Younger. Alma himself describes the influence of his father's
words on him:

And it came to pass that as I was thus racked with
torment, while I was harrowed up by the memory of
my many sins, behold, I remembered also to have
heard my father prophesy unto the people concerning
the coming of one Jesus Christ, a Son of God, to
atone for the sins of the world.

Now, as my mind caught hold upon this thought, I
cried within my heart: O Jesus, thou Son of God,
have mercy on me, who am in the gall of bitterness,
and am encircled about by the everlasting chains of
death. (Alma 36:17-18)

From this account it is very clear that Alma's father's testimony of Jesus Christ played a very important role in his
becoming reactivated after he had become an active apostate
(see Mosiah 27:8-9; Alma 36:6).

Once Alma the Younger became reactivated, he and the
sons of Mosiah, who were also reactivated, were able to
accomplish a great deal of good among their own people. The
following is an account of the missionary work of Alma and
the sons of Mosiah among the Nephites:

And they traveled throughout all the land of
Zarahemla, and among all the people who were under
the reign of King Mosiah, zealously striving to repair

all the injuries which they had done to the church, confessing all their sins, and publishing all the things which they had seen, and explaining the prophecies and the scriptures to all who desired to hear them.

And thus they were instruments in the hands of God in bringing many to the knowledge of the truth, yea, to the knowledge of their Redeemer.

And how blessed are they! For they did publish peace; they did publish good tidings of good; and they did declare unto the people that the Lord reigneth. (Mosiah 27:35-37)

Later these five young men helped convert thousands of Lamanites. Were it not for the words of righteous fathers, these young men most likely would have been lost forever.

Maintain an attitude that if you have consistently exercised your patriarchal keys in behalf of your children, at some point in their lives they will begin to cry to the Lord, even if they have been inactive for some period of time.

When wayward children begin to pray sincerely, the Lord softens their hearts and they heed their fathers' teachings. The testimony of President Spencer W. Kimball may strengthen your faith in this promise:

I have sometimes seen children of good families rebel, resist, stray, sin, and even actually fight God. In this they bring sorrow to their parents, who have done their best to set in movement a current and to teach and live as examples. But I have repeatedly seen many of these same children, after years of wandering, mellow, realize what they have been missing, repent, and make a great contribution to the spiritual life of their community. The reason I believe this can take place is that, despite all the adverse winds to which these people have been subjected, they have been influenced still more, and much more than they realized, by the current of life in the homes in which they were reared. When, in later years, they feel a longing to recreate in their own families the same

159

atmosphere they enjoyed as children, they are likely to turn to the faith that gave meaning to their parents' lives. (*Teachings of Spencer W. Kimball*, p. 335)

As a patriarch, you have the responsibility to exercise faith continually regarding the power and influence of your words on the lives of your children. Your faith is a key factor in the Holy Ghost bringing your teachings to the remembrance of your children. The Lord has promised he will bless your children according to your faith and desires (see Alma 29:4).

Invite Them Back

Last, as a patriarch follow the Lord's example in consistently inviting your wayward children back into full fellowship in your family. Reach out in a spirit of love. These invitations can be in conversations or letters. In some instances, you will find it much easier to express yourself in a letter. As a rule, expressions of love and desires in behalf of your wayward children will be more effective than preaching. When children are inactive, a cloud of darkness comes over their minds (see Helaman 5:34); they are not receptive to the truths of the gospel. Interestingly, when the right situation arises, the Lord will touch wayward children, and in many cases prompt them to repent (see Helaman 5:40-41). The classic example is the story of the prodigal son (see Luke 15:11-32).

You need to be realistic about how long it will take a wayward child to rise above his or her past mistakes. The following remarks by President Spencer W. Kimball call for a realistic perspective:

> The way of the transgressor is hard and tough and long and thorny. But the Lord has promised that for all those sins and errors outside of the named unpardonable sins, there is forgiveness. But sometimes it takes longer to climb back up the steep hill than it did to skid down it. And it is often much more difficult.
>
> When total self-conviction is stirred to a new life, and prayers have been multiplied, and fasting,

through humility, intensified, and weeping has been sanctified, repentance then begins to grow and eventually forgiveness may come. (*Teachings of Spencer W. Kimball*, p. 81)

Make every effort to be understanding, realizing that your wayward children will likely feel awkward when they first begin to think about returning to activity. Assure them that you will receive them with open arms and will be willing to assist them in any way you can. Above all else, let them know you are willing to forgive them. In turn, you as a patriarch should promise your children that the Lord will forgive them if they are willing to repent. Satan will do everything in his power to get wayward children to conclude there is no hope.

Your ability to help a wayward child will be limited unless you understand all of the factors that led to your child's inactivity. In some instances, the explanations are not obvious. In a sense they are mysterious. You need to trust the Lord's promise that he will help you understand mysteries regarding your child's lack of faith, etc. With insight and understanding you will be much more effective in helping a wayward child (see D&C 6:11).

Your yardstick in how you deal with wayward children, as compared with children who remain active in the church, should be the Lord's parable of the lost sheep.

> What man of you, having an hundred sheep, if he lose one of them, doth not leave the ninety in the wilderness, and go after that which is lost, until he find it?
>
> And when he hath found it, he layeth it on his shoulders, rejoicing.
>
> And when he cometh home, he calleth together his friends and neighbors, saying unto them, Rejoice with me; for I have found my sheep which was lost. (Luke 15:4-6)

Focus on the Lord's Glorious Promise

When wayward children return, the Lord has promised: "He who has repented of his sins, the same is forgiven, and I the Lord remember them no more" (D&C 58:42). As a father, you should never lose sight of this glorious promise: "I say unto you, there is joy in the presence of the angels of God over one sinner that repenteth" (Luke 15:10). If you as a father see one of your wayward children return to activity, you will discover there is a sweet joy in the reactivation. Then, and only then, will you fully understand the Lord's statement as recorded by Luke:

> I say unto you, that likewise joy shall be in heaven over one sinner that repenteth, more than over ninety and nine just persons, which need no repentance. (Luke 15:7)

12

Extend Your Influence as a Patriarch

Nephi's writings about his father Lehi illustrate another important lesson. From Nephi's writings we learn that under certain conditions, a man who holds the Melchizedek Priesthood can function as a patriarch in some respects for people other than his own family. We see Lehi acting as a patriarch in behalf of Zoram and his family, and the sons of Ishmael.

> And now, Zoram, I speak unto you; Behold, thou art the servant of Laban, nevertheless, thou hast been brought out of the land of Jerusalem, and I know that thou art a true friend unto my son, Nephi, forever.
>
> Wherefore, because thou hast been faithful thy seed shall be blessed with his seed, that they dwell in prosperity long upon the face of this land; and nothing, save it shall be iniquity among them, shall harm or disturb their prosperity upon the face of this land forever.
>
> Wherefore, if ye shall keep the commandments of the Lord, the Lord hath consecrated this land for the security of thy seed with the seed of my son. (2 Nephi 1:30-32)

• • •

> And it came to pass that when my father had made
> an end of speaking unto them, behold, he spake unto
> the sons of Ishmael, yea, and even all his household.
> (2 Nephi 4:10)

Full-Time Missionaries

Young men who serve as full-time missionaries for the church are set apart by their stake presidents. This ordination, coupled with their authority as holders of the Melchizedek Priesthood, gives them the authority to perform certain patriarchal functions in behalf of other people. While serving as full-time missionaries, young men have many opportunities to perform patriarchal functions in behalf of others. Unfortunately, some missionaries lack vision and exercise their authority only in conjunction with priesthood ordinances (baptisms, confirmations, etc.), failing to realize they have the authority to perform other patriarchal functions in behalf of the people they teach. In many ways, a mission provides a young man with an apprenticeship in fatherhood.

As you have sons, make every effort to help them see how their missions can provide them with vital training in performing their patriarchal duties as a father. Teach them to look for parallels between their work as a missionary and their later role as a patriarch to their own families. As you succeed in helping your sons see the similarities, they will approach their missions more conscientiously; and once they are married, they will have a much better grasp of their authority as a patriarch in their own home.

Extended Family

As a patriarch you can meet with your married children and their families, or on some occasions invite them to meet with you and your wife for an extended family counsel. In these meetings you can share perceptions, express concerns, command, admonish, teach, etc.

It is appropriate for your married children to request special blessings from you for themselves or in behalf of their children. Let your married children know you would be honored to respond to such a request. At the same time, never assume the role of the father in their home. Only give blessings to your married children or grandchildren by invitation.

If a mother is without a husband or her husband does not hold the priesthood and her father holds the priesthood, she could ask him to perform patriarchal functions in behalf of her children. If a mother does not understand the patriarchal keys of the priesthood, a bishop or home teacher could suggest this to her.

Home Teaching

In some situations home teachers can perform patriarchal duties in behalf of families they are assigned to visit. In those instances where there are children without fathers, or where their fathers do not hold the Melchizedek Priesthood, home teachers, under the direction of their bishop and priesthood leaders, have the authority and responsibility to function as patriarchs to some degree. Even though a mother can do many things to bless her children, the family will be limited unless patriarchal keys are exercised in family members' behalf. It is the Lord's desire that the blessings associated with the priesthood be extended into these homes.

Obviously a mother can do everything associated with the duties of a father as a patriarch, other than perform priesthood ordinances. Mothers without the priesthood in their homes have the assurance that the Lord will work through them to bless their children. However, mothers who do not have the priesthood in their home can invite home teachers to perform patriarchal functions in behalf of their children. If they do, home teachers will feel much more inclined to perform patriarchal duties for their family. For example, it would be appropriate for a mother without a husband to invite her home teachers to give a son a special blessing before he leaves home to go to school or into the military. Unless mothers make such a request, it is unlikely that home teachers will feel inclined to give the children special blessings.

Even in homes where fathers hold the priesthood, home teachers can be invited to leave a blessing in the home at the conclusion of a visit. If you have the opportunity to home teach with your sons, you should provide them with direction in how to bless a family as home teachers. Such experiences as home teaching help sons prepare themselves to be patriarchs as fathers.

Do Not Overstep the Bounds of Your Authority

As a holder of the Melchizedek Priesthood, you need to be very careful not to overstep the bounds of your authority outside your own home. Any efforts on your part in behalf of others should be performed under the direction of presiding priesthood officers. Otherwise you will be guilty of unrighteous dominion even if you are well-intentioned.

The Lord's House is a house of order, and every function of the priesthood should be performed within the bounds the Lord has stipulated. For example, even though you hold the priesthood, you do not have the authority to baptize or ordain one of your own children without the authorization of the bishop. There are certain things a bishop cannot do without the authorization of the stake president. There are some functions in the priesthood a stake president cannot perform without authorization from the General Authorities of the church.

It is important that you never lose sight of the order of the priesthood in your efforts to extend your influence as a patriarch beyond your own family. At the same time, you should strive to be sensitive to the promptings of the spirit in extending your influence as a patriarch beyond your family. The Lord has declared that it is the responsibility of those who hold the priesthood to bless others (see Gen. 12:3; Gen. 18:18; Gal. 3:8).

Benevolent Service

Even though all the saving ordinances of the gospel of Jesus Christ require the power of the priesthood, many human needs can be met through benevolent service independent of the priesthood. Your sense of fulfillment in this life will not be complete unless you are involved in rendering such service. Of all the things we can do to serve God, service to others is the most efficacious. King Benjamin understood this profound truth:

> And behold, I tell you these things that ye may learn wisdom; that ye may learn that when ye are in the service of your fellow beings ye are only in the service of your God. (Mosiah 2:17)

Following are some of the commandments the Lord has given regarding your responsibility to render benevolent service to people:

> For the poor shall never cease out of the land: therefore I command thee, saying, Thou shalt open thine hand wide unto thy brother, to thy poor, and to thy needy, in thy land. (Deut. 15:11)

• • •

> Therefore, strengthen your brethren in all your conversations, in all your prayers, in all your exhortations, and in all your doings. (D&C 108:7)

• • •

> And also, ye yourselves will succor those that stand in need of your succor; ye will administer of your substance unto him that standeth in need; and ye will not suffer that the beggar putteth up his petition to you in vain, and turn him out to perish. (Mosiah 4:16)

• • •

> And now, for the sake of these things which I have spoken unto you—that is, for the sake of retaining a remission of your sins from day to day, that ye may

walk guiltless before God—I would that ye should impart of your substance to the poor, every man according to that which he hath, such as feeding the hungry, clothing the naked, visiting the sick, and administering to their relief, both spiritually and temporally, according to their wants. (Mosiah 4:26)

• • •

Let your hearts be full, drawn out in prayer unto him continually for . . . the welfare of those around you. (Alma 34:27)

• • •

Behold, I say unto you, that ye must visit the poor and the needy and administer to their relief, that they may be kept until all things may be done, according to my law which ye have received. (D&C 44:6)

• • •

And remember in all things the poor and the needy, the sick and the afflicted, for he that doeth not these things, the same is not my disciple. (D&C 52:10)

In speaking to those that hold the priesthood, President Gordon B. Hinkley said:

To every officer, to every teacher in this Church who acts in a priesthood office, there comes the sacred responsibility of magnifying that priesthood calling. Each of us is responsible for the welfare and the growth and development of others. We do not live only unto ourselves. If we are to magnify our callings, we cannot love only unto ourselves. As we serve with diligence, as we teach with faith and testimony, as we lift and strengthen and build convictions of righteousness in those whose lives we touch, we magnify our priesthood. To love only unto ourselves, on the other hand, to serve grudgingly, to give less than our best effort to our duty, diminishes our priesthood just as looking through the wrong lenses of binoculars reduces the image and makes more distant the object. (*Ensign*, May 1989, p. 47)

In his writing President Spencer W. Kimball noted several things that can be accomplished through such service:

> One is measuring up to his opportunity potential when he has saved a crumbling marriage, transformed the weak into the strong, changed a civil to a proper temple marriage, brought enemies from the cesspool of hate to the garden of love, made a child trust and love him, changed a scoffer into a worshiper, melted a stony heart into one of flesh and muscle. (*Teachings of Spencer W. Kimball*, pp. 249-250)

From the scriptures we learn that the Lord is displeased with those who do not render benevolent service:

> Yea, he saw great inequality among the people, some lifting themselves up with their pride, despising others, turning their backs upon the needy and the naked and those who were hungry, and those who were athirst, and those who were sick and afflicted.
>
> Now this was a great cause for lamentations among the people, while others were abasing themselves, succoring those who stood in need of their succor, such as imparting their substance to the poor and the needy, feeding the hungry, and suffering all manner of afflictions, for Christ's sake, who should come according to the spirit of prophecy. (Alma 4:12-13)

• • •

> Yea, and will you persist in turning your backs upon the poor, and the needy, and in withholding your substance from them? (Alma 5:55)

• • •

> For behold, ye do love money, and your substance, and your fine apparel, and the adorning of your churches, more than ye love the poor and the needy, the sick and the afflicted.

Why do ye adorn yourselves with that which hath no
life, and yet suffer the hungry, and the needy, and the
naked, and the sick and the afflicted to pass by you,
and notice them not? (Mormon 8:37, 39)

• • •

And they did impart of their substance, every man
according to that which he had, to the poor, and the
needy, and the sick, and the afflicted; and they did
not wear costly apparel, yet they were neat and come-
ly. (Alma 1:27)

In some instances, your experience as a patriarch to your
family will assist you in meeting human needs that are not
associated with saving ordinances. For example, this experience can assist you in counseling friends or acquaintances. It
could assist you in being especially insightful in cheering up
those that are discouraged, comforting people in times of sorrow, or being a friend to someone in need. As you conscientiously perform your patriarchal duties, you will be more
receptive to the promptings of the spirit regarding the needs
of others.

As a result of your callings in the priesthood, you will have
numerous opportunities to help people cope with fears, frustrations, and personal problems. You will experience a sense
of joy when you see these same individuals achieve peace and
stability in their lives.

The Lord's promise to Joseph Smith regarding the joy associated with seeing someone converted also applies to
strengthening members of the church:

Now how great is his joy in the soul that repenteth!

Wherefore, you are called to cry repentance unto this
people.

And if it so be that you should labor all your days in
crying repentance unto this people, and [strengthen]
save it be one soul . . . how great shall be your joy
with him in the kingdom of my Father.

And now, if your joy will be great with one soul that
you have [strengthened] . . . how great will be your
joy if you should [strengthen] . . . many souls. (D&C
18:13-16)

Being a true Christian in your relationship with other people is the essence of the gospel of Jesus Christ. As you lift and
assist others, God will lift and assist you:

Only when you lift a burden, God will lift your burden. . . . The man who staggers and falls because his
burden is too great can lighten that burden by taking
on the weight of another's burden. You get by giving,
but your part of giving must be given first. (Spencer
W. Kimball, *Teachings of Spencer W. Kimball*, p. 251)

In the Lord's scheme your needs will be met by others for
the most part. Commenting on this basic truth, President
Spencer W. Kimball said: "But it is usually through another
mortal that he meets our needs" (*Teachings of Spencer W.
Kimball*, p. 252).

Never underestimate your power of influence for good.
Even the simplest acts of service and encouragement can
result in glorious consequences, especially when the spirit of
love accompanies your efforts. Strive to give of your time and
self freely—and your means according to your circumstances.
As you do, the quality of your life will be greatly enhanced.
You will discover that giving of yourself and your means is the
key to your finding the abundant life.

As you make an effort to assist others with their trials and
problems, it will help you put your own challenges in their
proper perspective:

When we are engaged in the service of our fellowmen, not only do our deeds assist them, but we put
our own problems in a fresher perspective. When we
concern ourselves more with others, there is less time
to be concerned with ourselves. In the midst of the
miracle of serving, there is the promise of Jesus, that
by losing ourselves, we find ourselves. (Spencer W.
Kimball, *Teachings of Spencer W. Kimball*, p. 254)

As a holder of the priesthood, you should never lose sight of the caution expressed by President Spencer W. Kimball regarding service:

> Too often in the past, organizational lines in the Church have become walls that have kept us from reaching out to individuals as completely as we should. We will also find that as we become less concerned with getting organizational or individual credit, we will become more concerned with serving the one whom we are charged to reach. We will also find ourselves concerned with our true and ultimate identity as a son or daughter of our Father in Heaven, and helping others to achieve the same sense of belonging. (*Teachings of Spencer W. Kimball*, p. 256)

Never become so busy in performing your formal priesthood assignments that you have no time left for simple service to neighbors or acquaintances. There is a difference between holding and magnifying the priesthood. Magnifying your priesthood involves more than completing priesthood assignments. To magnify your priesthood you must consistently increase your ability to bless and assist others. As you are faithful in magnifying your priesthood, the Lord has promised that you will be sanctified by the spirit (see D&C 84:33). As this happens, "you shall live by every word that proceedeth forth from the mouth of God" (D&C 84:44).